The
DARK SIDE
of the
Purpose Driven
Church

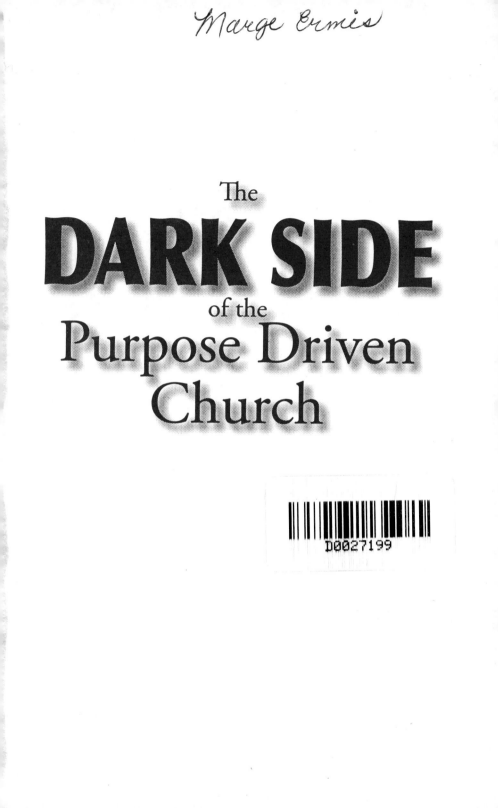

D0027199

© 2005, 2007 by Noah W. Hutchings. All rights reserved. No part of this book may be used or reproduced in any manner whatsoever without written permission of the publisher, except in the case of brief quotations in articles and reviews. For more information write: Bible Belt Publishing, P.O. Box 100, Bethany, OK 73008, 1-800-652-1144, *www.swrc.com.*

Printed in the United States of America

ISBN 1-933641-00-2

The

DARK SIDE

of the

Purpose Driven Church

Noah W. Hutchings

Contents

Introduction

And have no fellowship with the unfruitful works of darkness, but rather reprove them.

—Ephesians 5:11

The night is far spent, the day is at hand: let us therefore cast off the works of darkness, and let us put on the armour of light.

—Romans 13:12

In the epistles to the churches there are twenty-one exhortations for Christians to abolish the works of darkness in their fellowship and service. In almost each one of his epistles Paul cautioned the churches to be alert to that darkness which would extinguish the light of the Gospel and dim their testimony.

The title of this book, *The Dark Side of the Purpose Driven Church*, has a special warning to Christians today. Perhaps the greatest paradigm shift that has visited the church since the Protestant Reformation ignited by Martin Luther may be occurring at the present time in the purpose driven church movement birthed by Dr. Rick Warren. Pastor Warren in his seeming initial success in attracting thousands of the unchurched to attend and join his church that was using revolutionary evangelical approaches, warranted praises from some of the highest theological voices in the nation. Tens of thousands of pastors have heeded his advice through Internet counseling and regional seminars.

Dr. Warren's articles have appeared in major magazines worldwide; he has appeared on the most popular television talk shows; some thirty million of his books have been purchased by church members; and thousands of churches worldwide have used his forty-day outreach programs. Dr. Warren has proposed a world peace plan that involves sending one billion church members into the nations to eliminate war, hunger, disease, and injustice. Of course, if Dr. Warren is successful, then we can delete about half the Bible and send a radiogram to Jesus that He doesn't need to come back to destroy those who would destroy the world (Rev. 11).

I was a member of a community church that had grown from a mission in 1975 to the number two Southern Baptist Church in Oklahoma by 2002. It was a community, family, evangelical, fundamental, soul-winning church. In 2004 there were so many children, including teenagers, it was difficult to get from the educational building to the main assembly building. Decisions for Christ were made at every church service.

The church staff, at least the pastor and a few chosen others, had gone to Saddleback to take Dr. Warren's seminars on church growth. Why, I have no idea. In 2002 the church music began to change, and I know a few began to leave, but the choir, piano, and church orchestra was left untouched, for the most part. The new pastor came and all the changes I listed in my tract began to take place. I asked one of the head deacons what was going on, and he responded, "Oh, there are going to be great changes in the church." I asked again, "What's broke?" I stayed six months until what appeared to be only about half the membership remained, and then I left. Although the pastor has since gone back to a more traditional worship, the church is only a shadow of its former self. Two of the three parking lots and areas seem to be always empty when I pass by on the way to my present church. Rick Warren trashed my church.

Our ministry reaches from New England to California, from

Alaska to Florida, and from the reports I have received from our listenership, the PDC program may occasionally result in membership growth, but in nine out of ten cases, the result is negative or fatal. Many churches where souls were being saved are now saving fewer or none at all after going purpose driven. The question now is not how many are being saved in purpose driven churches, but how many are going to Hell because of the PDC movement. I wonder if the adage "He's crying all the way to the bank" applies?

Certainly, churches need changes and new programs to adjust to urban congestion, secular entertainment, social and moral attractions and distractions, but to try to force pastors and church staffs to use Dr. Warren's plan that worked in a special situation at a certain time is like trying to sell refrigerators to Eskimos, or water wings to Sahara bedouins.

Dr. Warren has hundreds of pungent one-liners in his book *The Purpose Driven Church,* and additional hundreds of strained scriptural applications in his book *The Purpose Driven Life.* But getting it all together is like trying to put forty buckets of honey into a barrel with your hands, or tying a bucket or red worms together to make one continual string.

Whatever may be said of me or this book, one thing that cannot be said is that I didn't try the spirits of the PDC movement as commanded in 1 John 4:1–4.

Since the first printing of this book in 2005, there have been several printings due to the number of requests and orders from bookstores. In this update, July 2007, I have made several revisions and added several chapters. However, even though thousands of letters and e-mails from constituents could have been added, this would have resulted in adding thousands of pages. All these added letters and e-mails, besides the thousands of calls from listeners around the world, have all related practically the same stories about what occurred in their churches when the purpose driven program was initiated or introduced. Therefore, the letters as included in the 2005 original edition have been left as they were.

Inasmuch as Dr. Rick Warren has stated repeatedly that he has personally trained over four hundred thousand pastors and ministers, and reached millions more through his books and other means of communication, he must be given credit for the purpose driven church phenomenon that is filling the world. But credit also entails responsibility. Methods cannot be divorced from the message. And every pastor or minister is commanded to try the spirits, whether they be of God or another source.

Chapter One

Marginalized by Proxy

In early 1998 my awareness or concerns about the church growth move-ment, and the purpose driven church in particular, were peripheral at best. If someone had mentioned Saddleback Church, I probably would have thought it was a church youth camp in Wyoming. My ignorance was suddenly jolted with the publication of a book titled *End-Time Visions: The Road to Armageddon?* by Richard Abanes, a member of Saddleback and evidently an associate of Dr. Warren, pos-sibly an employee of the church. The book, surprisingly, was published by Broadman & Holman Publishers, a d/b/a of the Southern Baptist Sunday School Board. In this book, I was viciously slandered, evidently because I believed in the visible pre-millennial return of Jesus Christ. Not only was I trashed, but so were many other pastors, ministers, and authors who were of like understanding of biblical eschatology. In speaking with some of the SBC powers-that-be at Nashville, it was my understanding that they sought justification in the publishing of the book because it had been recommended by Dr. Rick Warren.

When I requested that the Southern Baptist Convention move to write me a letter of apology and remove Abanes' book from circulation, I was in effect told to go jump in the lake. Subsequent to this advice, I responded by making my indignation public in our October 1998 newsletter, *The Prophetic Observer,* and presented two programs on the subject over the broadcast. Because some who read this book may not have read this article, I am reprinting it in part in this first chapter.

Southern Baptist Sunday School Board: Vision Or Venom?

If a man say, I love God, and hateth his brother, he is a liar: for he that loveth not his brother whom he hath seen, how can he love God whom he hath not seen?

—1 John 4:20

Doth a fountain send forth at the same place sweet water and bitter?

—James 3:11

Lie *(v.)*: to make an untrue statement with intent to deceive; to create a false or misleading impression.

Lie *(n.)*: An assertion of something known or believed by the speaker to be untrue with intent to deceive; an untrue or inaccurate statement that may or may not be believed true by the speaker; something that misleads or deceives.

Libel: A written or oral defamatory statement or representation that conveys an unjustly unfavorable impression; a statement or representation published without just cause and tending to expose another to public contempt; defamation of a person by written or representational means.

Slander: The utterance of false charges or misrepresentations which defame or damage another's reputation.

—*Webster's New Collegiate Dictionary*

While attending the Christian Booksellers Convention in Dallas, I purchased a book by Broadman & Holman Publishers. The title is *End-Time Visions: The Road to Armageddon?* by Richard Abanes, 428 pages, copyrighted 1998, with a retail price of $25.95. On the cover leaf is a brief bio about the author:

> The director of the Religious Information Center in Southern California, Richard Abanes is himself a former cult member (The Way International). He is regarded by organizations as diverse as the FBI, the Simon Wiesenthal Center, the Southern Poverty Law Center, and the U.S. Bureau of Alcohol, Tobacco, and Firearms, as an authority on the religious and political fringe.

The bio also refers to other books by Abanes and news media outlets on which he has made guest appearances. The inference from the bio immediately calls the reader's attention to the assumption that the personalities discussed within the book are those on either the religious or political "fringe" who may need to be under scrutiny by Abanes for the FBI or the BATF, especially so since no qualification is offered.

I was naturally interested, because Noah Hutchings and Southwest Radio Church are mentioned several times in the book, involving approximately forty statements presented as facts, truths, or widely known opinions. Even so, I would have simply filed the book for future reference had not the publisher been the SBC Sunday School Board d/b/a Broadman & Holman Publishers. Some of the other Christian ministers or ministries dealt with in the book are: David Allen Lewis, J. R. Church, Terry Cook, Hal Lindsey, Dave Breese, Chuck Missler, Harold Camping, Tim LaHaye, Peter LaLonde, Charles Taylor, Grant Jeffrey, Salem Kirban, Don McAlvany, Pat Robertson, John Hagee, Jack Van Impe, and others. Those listed in the political and religious "fringe," and their activities discussed, include a multitude of seers, psychics, survivalists, militia, and terrorists: Marshall Applewhite, Jim Jones, Jehovah's Witnesses, Mormons, David Koresh, Nostradamus, Randy Weaver, Hart Armstrong, Louis Farrakhan, Timothy McVeigh, Jeanne Dixon, and others too numerous to mention. I was somewhat surprised not to find the names of Atilla the Hun, Jack the Ripper, and Jeffrey Dahmer, although I did locate our inclusive relationship to the Emperor Nero. The author puts everyone in the same category—the religious and political fringe. Abanes' references to Christian ministers mentioned in his book is with the same disdain and utter contempt that he writes about Jim Jones, David Koresh, and terrorists.

It was somewhat disconcerting to learn that I was being slandered by a d/b/a of the SBC Sunday School Board after serving for forty years in SBC churches. Therefore, following scriptural guidelines, I wrote Broadman & Holman a letter and sent it special delivery with a return receipt requested. In the letter I pointed out that:

> . . . In every reference to me or the ministry I represent they have been taken out of context, an exaggerated meaning is applied, the statement is based on the author's opinion and presented as fact, or the statement is a total lie.

I listed seven of the statements in the book that would fall within this category. In my letter I requested:

> Please consider the immediate removal of this book from circulation, as well as a written apology and retraction. . . . I would advise you that I have discussed this matter with counsel, and a response is needed by September 1, 1998.

We in Christian communications ministries cannot be detracted by every barking dog, but his book would go to all Baptist Book Stores, be read by thousands of pastors and church members, and the publisher gave the book some respectability and seeming credibility. I called the local Baptist Book Store, but the book had been on back order for two months because the sales were so heavy. On September 1, I received a reply by fax from William D. Watkins, senior acquisitions and development editor.

We received your August 13, 1998, letter stating your concern over our publication of a book by Richard Abanes entitled "End-Time Visions: The Road to Armageddon?" In this letter, you ask us "to please consider the immediate removal of this book from circulation, as well as [supply] a written apology and retraction." We have discussed this matter with the book's author, as well as with our legal counsel, and we have determined that the references to you and to Southwest Radio Church in the book "End-Time Visions" are expressions of opinion or comment made by the author or cited by him upon publicly made statements and writings. Such comments and opinions are allowed and protected by law. Therefore, we respectfully decline your request for a removal of the book from our publishing line, and we have decided not to offer any apology or retraction.

The book's author, Richard Abanes, is a highly respected investigative reporter and well-known author was also serves part-time at Rick Warren's church in Southern California. Mr. Abanes is a Southern Baptist in good standing, and he is an individual with whom I have known and been associated with for several years now.

Broadman & Holman has a licensing agreement with the New York-based publisher Four Walls Eight Windows in which we distribute the book to the Christian market while Four Walls Eight Windows sells the books to the general public. Prior to the books' publication, we reviewed the book for typographical errors and for any content concerns. We stood behind the book then, and we do so now.

Respectfully,
William D. Watkins

If a d/b/a of the SBC Sunday School Board wants to back Richard Abanes as the self-appointed sheriff of Heaven, that is their business—but not at my expense. In this book I was condemned as a doomsayer, a datesetter, a fearmonger, and placed in the category of a multitude of reprobates who are surely on their way to Hell. Therefore, I reference just a few of the statements about me included in the book.

. . . . .

This practice of using a qualifying "?" has become a classic technique used by date-suggesters. (p. 101)

Response: Abanes complained that Southwest Radio Church uses question marks to suggest dates for the Second Coming. This complaint was in references we made to the last generation spoken of by Jesus in relation to the return of a Jewish remnant to the land. We simply asked would a generation be forty years? fifty years? seventy years? and when was the last generation to begin, in 1948? in 1967? etc. It is strange that Abanes would complain about the use of question marks when his own book's title is *End-Time Visions: The Road to Armageddon?*

. . . . .

SRC inherited this doomsday philosophy from David Webber's father, Dr. Edward F. Webber, who founded SRC. The elder Webber gained his own reputation as an end-time prophet in the 1940s by suggesting that Hitler was the Antichrist. (p. 101)

Response: Many ministers during World War II suggested that Hitler might be the Antichrist. He had risen up out of the old Roman Empire; he had plans to conquer the world; he purposed to kill every Jew; his Panzer divisions were headed toward Jerusalem; he had made a concordat with the pope. However, Dr. Webber never mentioned to me that he thought Hitler was the Antichrist, and I have never read anything he wrote where he said Hitler was the Antichrist.

. . . . .

Gaverluk suggested that Mars might actually be thrown out of orbit and sent plummeting toward Earth. (p. 100)

Response: Abanes calls this suggestion by Dr. Gaverluk a "fanciful tale." However, Immanuel Velikovsky in *Earth in Upheaval,* and Donald Wesley Patten in *Catastrophism and the Old Testament,* as well as several others, have suggested the very thing as possibly happening in the past and as being a threat in the future. If research instead of slander had been the principle motivation, Abanes would have at least amended his statement.

. . . . .

Closely connected to this fanciful tale is the theory put forth by both Webber and Hutchings that "hell" may be either a white dwarf star somewhere or a black hole. . . . At the same time, Hutchings and Webber have suggested that hell may be housed on Venus. (p. 368)

Response: If Abanes had actually read my book, *Apocalyptic Signs in the Heavens,* which he claims to have done, then he knowingly made deceitful claims. If he simply used Bill Alnor's references in *Soothsayers of the Second Advent,* then he might plead ignorance. However, a person who disseminates an untruth, even unknowingly, is just as guilty as the original source.

The explanation of a nova meltdown resulting in a white dwarf star or a black hole, as quoted in our book, was from *Relativity and Cosmology* by William J. Kaufman III. The comparison to the "lake of fire" was originally made by Dr. C. T. Schwarze of New York University. The complete scientific comparison is quoted in full in my book, so Abanes is without excuse. Hundreds of authors and ministers have used this illustration to explain what Hell, or the lake of fire, may be like. As far as Abanes' claim that we said Hell was on Venus, I quote exactly what I wrote in *Apocalyptic Signs in the Heavens:*

> A more detailed description of Venus was provided in a NASA release that appeared in the October 24, 1966, edition of the *Daily Oklahoma:* "Venus is a 'hell hole' with fiery storms raging in a metal-melting atmosphere so dense light can't escape. . . ." It is amazing that our own space agency had to resort to Bible terminology to report what is being discovered in outer space.

Again, Abanes is revealed as being interested more in slander that in serious objective research. I would think that some heads would roll at Broadman & Holman and the SBCSS Board.

. . . . .

> Another Fundamentalist Christian—Noah Hutchings of the Southwest Radio Church—had dogmatically labeled AIDS "the worst plague in history."

Response: Baloney! Abanes references me by some person I have never heard of in all my years in the ministry, and what difference does it make anyway? If Abanes wants to think that jock itch is the greatest plague in history, that is fine with me.

There is much disagreement as to the future spread of AIDS and whether HIV mutations will spread. UNAIDS (*1997 World Almanac*) reports that in mid-1996, 27.9 million people had contracted AIDS, and that 62 percent of the inhabitants of sub-Sahara Africa had contracted AIDS. I recently visited an AIDS compound in Havana and consulted with AIDS researchers there where the AIDS strain was affecting males and females equally. I probably know as much or more about AIDS as Abanes or anyone at the SBCSS Board.

In any event, Abanes made this statement just to make another try at discrediting me. In doing so, he referenced four sources to try to prove that the Black Death, and not AIDS, is the greatest plague in history. But even here, the great researcher Abanes goofed. All four sources quoted were dated between 1969 and 1983.

I could continue to reference every statement made about me or the ministry in *End-Time Visions,* but there is no more space. But not one... not a single one... is accurate. I do not know if statements made about other ministers and ministries in the book are accurate or not, but I would assume the pattern would be much the same.

The references to me and the ministry in *End-Time Visions* were made to damage my reputation, made to defame me personally, and made to financially damage the Southwest Radio Church. Surely the Southern Baptist Sunday School Board d/b/a Broadman & Holman Publishers should be held responsible, as they affirm that Richard Abanes is a highly respected investigative reporter, that he is their friend, and that they stand behind all content in his book.

I am confident that most of the Christian ministries and ministers who have been the object of religious McCarthyism in *End-Time Visions* will meekly submit without responding—afraid to challenge the ecclesiastical bureaucrats sitting in ivory towers in Nashville. One thing I have never been accused of being is a coward, and at seventy-five I am too old to change now. If Broadman & Holman and/or the SBC Sunday School Board wants to dispute the pre-mil, pre-trib prophetic position of the segment of ministers who feel called of God to biblically interpret the signs of the times, then let both entities produce an open, honest, and credible work, and not hide behind something that in my opinion is even lower than the *National Enquirer.*

. . . . .

We assume that Dr. Rick Warren, by proxy, attempted to marginalize all ministers and pre-mil theologians who would dare to disagree doctrinally with his obviously A-millennial persuasions. Richard Abanes is obviously still in close fellowship with Dr. Warren, as his defense of the purpose driven church religion continues in his latest book, *Rick Warren and the Purpose That Drives Him,* published by Harvest House Publishers, copyright 2005, released in July of 2005. This book, on the back cover, notes of Richard Abanes, "A nationally recognized authority on cults and religions." In our opinion, Richard Abanes himself is a member of the most pervasive cult to ever invade the church.

It should be noted by the reader that after the publication of our October 1998 newsletter, we received a call from Mr. William D. Watkins to inform me that the book by Richard Abanes, *End-Time Visions: The Road to Armageddon?* was being withdrawn from circulation and the uncirculated stock would be "remaindered." It was also announced subsequently by Broadman & Holman that Mr. Watkins had resigned to accept a "higher position."

In the 1940s and 1950s, with the expanding teaching of evolution in the public schools from K-1 to university levels, including seminaries, there was presented to various Bible societies and publishers capitalistic opportunities to market new Bible versions from the 1881 Greek New Testament taken from the Alexandrian texts. Subsequently, the opinions and traditions of men took over, resulting in an explosion of new theologies like the social gospel, the "God Is Dead" theology, searching for the historical Jesus, existentialism, New Age mysticism, etc.

Mac Dominick, president of the Procom Group, seems to have summed up the consensus of this gathering religious smog that hung over the nation the last half of the twentieth century in his new book, *Rebuilding the Tower of Babel,* chapter one, "Angel of Light":

The members of every past generation embraced the notion that their time was the pivotal point in human history, and to varying degrees, each one has been correct in this assessment. This concept applies not only to secular society and humanity in general, but also to specific segments of the world's population; and the present world population is no exception to this mentality. In the context of this manuscript, the world's occult and Christian populations are both acutely cognizant of the fact of humanity's position at the climax of the current "age" and are endowed with a distinct sense of revolutionary, imminent change.

As a prime example, in a 1989 speech to the Association of Supervision and Curriculum Development, Dr. Jean Houston was dogmatic that this very generation will determine whether the human race will grow to a new, heightened level of consciousness or annihilate itself. In this speech she stated: "All cultures thought their culture was 'it.' They were wrong, this is 'it'—this time in history . . . the great 'time of either/or.' . . . Everything is in place to make the leap, the jump phenomenon. . . . We are living the passion of the loaded time . . . when what you and I do will profoundly make a difference."

Dr. Houston went on to speak of a "whole system transition to a planetary society." Her definition of a planetary society is quite simple: a planetary society is based on an interdependent central-ized social democracy that encompasses an entire human race whose collective consciousness will expand to the point that each individual realizes that he or she is, in fact, "god." This very mindset and mantra spans the course of paganism, Wicca, New Age, and other earth-based religions that comprise a major segment of what is deemed the "occult world."

On the other end of the spectrum, the members of the church are convinced that this indeed is a critical, pivotal moment in human history. Those who are dispensational in their theology and hold to a literal interpretation of Scripture believe that the "end of the age" that will consummate with the Rapture of the church, the kingdom of Antichrist, and the subsequent Second Coming is very close. In addition, the events seen as the obvious fulfillment of Bible prophecy that began in 1948 with the establishment of Israel as a nation continue to occur.

Imbedded into this ideological framework is also the realization that the church of Jesus Christ is facing a major shift away from the "Old Time Religion" of its fathers and grandfathers. This shift is not a minor adjustment, but rather, a major change that threatens to alter the face of Christianity forever. Tragically, if this shift continues unchecked, the subsequent change will create a new "hybrid Christianity" that will bear little resemblance to the "faith of our fathers" or the church as described in the New Testament. This new hybrid is instead birthing a "false Christianity" that will lead its adherents to a pseudo-faith that will result in their missing the Rapture, believing "a lie" and falling into the arms of Antichrist as gently as the falling petals of an autumn rose.

Rising up from the New Age ashes of pseudo-Christianity was one Robert Schuller, with his own heaven-on-earth blueprint, the Crystal Palace. The magical words to unlock the gate to the new dream Jerusalem was that salvation is within your own mind. The new gospel according to Schuller was improved upon by Dr. Rick Warren, marketed by Rupert Murdoch, and sold to ambitious but deceived church leaders around the world as the purpose driven church. Dr. Warren has come up with a formula that would finally bring all denominations together—make everyone think there is something in it just for them. Referencing Mac Dominick again, from his book *Outcome Based Religion:*

> ➢ Perception must be changed from viewing people as "saved" or "lost" to "churched" and "unchurched."

- ➤ "Find out what impresses the unchurched in your community" and do it.
- ➤ Bring in popular "heroes" to attract the multitudes.
- ➤ Use the successful principles of retailing: accessibility, surplus parking, inventory, service, visibility, and good cash flow.
- ➤ Pastors should model themselves after businessmen and plan strategically.
- ➤ "Do not preach expository sermons, you have to win them and build relationships."
- ➤ Move from a theocentric approach to ministry to a "human needs approach."
- ➤ "We must begin to say, 'I am not trying to convert any other religious people to my viewpoint.'"
- ➤ "There is no need for one to recognize his own personal sin, no need for repentance, no need for the crucifixion of self."
- ➤ "The Christ Spirit dwells in every human being."
- ➤ "Nothing exists except God."
- ➤ "Christ was self-esteem incarnate."
- ➤ "The most destructive thing that can be done to a person is to call him a sinner."
- ➤ "Sin is any act or thought that robs myself or another human being of his or her self-esteem."
- ➤ Rick Warren is also a graduate of Schuller's leadership conference.
- ➤ Robert Schuller's name appears on the endorsement pages of Rick Warren's book *The Purpose Driven Church*. Here Schuller states, "I am praying that every pastor will read this book, believe it . . . and change to match its sound, scriptural wisdom."
- ➤ In his book *The Purpose Driven Church*, Rick Warren notes, "I had not been in Southern California long before I realized it was an area that already had many strong, Bible–believing churches. Some of the best-known pastors in America ministered within

driving distance of our new church . . . Robert Schuller, . . . John Wimber, Jack Hayford. . . ."

➤ Robert Schuller's 1995 "Hour of Power" Seminar for Success for Churches six-video series includes videos by Bill Hybels, Rick Warren, Robert Schuller, David Yongi Cho, and Bill Wilson.

Chapter 2

Piggyback/Saddleback

I accepted Jesus Christ as my Saviour by faith in April 1951. I was a member of a local conservative and fundamental church in Oklahoma City until 1960 when I became a member of the First Baptist Church of Nicoma Park. I taught Sunday school and training union in that church until 1988. I did mission work at Northwest Baptist Church in Oklahoma City for a year, then my wife and I moved into a new neighborhood and moved our letter to a church near our new home. I am not giving the name of the church because it is not my intention to cause the pastor, even though I might have some negative feelings toward him, nor any of my friends who may still remain in the church, any embarrassment.

The church had been a mission in the mid-'70s, but by the time we had joined it was a fairly large church with a membership of three or four thousand and still growing. When I asked for an audience with the associate pastor, he remarked that my name was familiar. Then he opened a large drawer in a filing cabinet and it was packed full of articles and books that I had written. Evidently he had been a faithful listener to our broadcast for many years. I later served on the deacon board and as a substitute teacher in Sunday school. It was a joyful, evangelistic, friendly, community-serving church.

We could hardly get from the main educational building to the main assembly building between Sunday school and worship service for the many teenagers in the halls. Dr. Claude Thomas, the pastor, and I had a cordial and friendly relationship. Dr. Thomas left in about 1992 or 1993 for a pastorate in the Dallas area and Dr. Calvin Miller was the interim pastor for about two years. He was a professor at Southwestern University in Fort Worth, but would fly up on the weekend. Although Dr. Miller is most unusual in that you never know what he is going to say or do next, he and Mrs. Miller visited in our home and we had great fellowship. I am not dropping names to enhance this book, as I doubt that either Dr. Thomas or Dr. Miller will approve of what I am writing in this book. I have had several well known ministers commend us for the information we have disseminated about the purpose driven church, but when I ask them if they would care to be on our program when we address this subject, almost without exception they will say, "Oh, I would like to, but I can't take the chance."

Finally, the search committee enticed Dr. Mark Hartman to leave his church in Houston and accept the pastorate at my church. Dr. Hartman served wonderfully, a fine pulpit presenter, pre-mil, pre-trib. The membership continued to expand and not only did the huge parking lot fill up on Sunday, but so did two new five-acre parking lots to the north and west fill up. In 2002 it was announced that our church was the second largest Baptist church in Oklahoma. I served on the deacon board for five years, but due to being so busy at Southwest Radio Church and out of town on meetings and foreign tours and missions, I asked to be dropped; consequently, I was not privy to church business news other than that reported at regular open business meetings.

At some point in 2002 and into 2003 there appeared to be a change in church music and congregational song selections. There was a move to praise choruses and in choir selections that seemed disharmonic and loud. The minister of music had been at the church for over twenty years and when someone asked Dr. Hartman about the change, he remarked that it would remain the same. On another occasion Dr. Hartman said that this was a purpose driven church now. At the time, I really didn't know what it meant or if this was not just a slip of the tongue. Nothing else seemed to change.

In the fall of 2003 Dr. Hartman announced that he was resigning to take a church in the Houston area. It could have been that his contract with the church was for seven years, and he and his family desired to move back to Houston. Dr. Anthony Jordan, former pastor of Northwest Baptist Church who was now president of the Oklahoma Baptist Association, came as interim pastor. As far as sermon content and delivery, Dr. Jordan has no peers. Church business and growth continued.

Within a few weeks it was announced the church would have a general meeting to select a new search committee. When the meeting took place, the names of seven appeared on a printed ballot, which was somewhat unusual. It was explained that these were men who had already been examined for qualifications and were available. My name was not on the ballot, which was okay with me as I could not serve anyway. However, there were some questions, and the membership was told if they wanted to appoint someone else the additions would have to be nominated. I was nominated and received some votes, but of course, the majority simply checked the names already printed. It was obvious the committee was specially picked. In a few weeks it was announced the committee had selected a pastor for the church's approval. When I asked one of the deacons about the new pastor, he just smiled and said there were going to be great changes. When I asked about which changes, he just smiled and left.

On a Saturday before the church was to vote, there was a reception where the membership could meet the proposed new pastor, hear him speak, and ask him questions. As I remember, the vote took place on the following Sunday evening service. I had already decided that this dude from Texas was bad news, but he had been praised to the skies by the minister of music and the search committee as a combination of Martin Luther, Charles Spurgeon, and Billy Graham. The vote was announced by one of the search committee: "Of the 1,881 who voted, 1,871 want you as our pastor." This meant that ten voted no. I was one of the ten. The minister of music held up his Bible and said, "Two years ago I wrote in my Bible who would be the next pastor of this church." It was the name of the new pastor. Within a few days, the minister of music, the new pastor, and a select few went to the Willow Creek Church in Chicago for purpose driven church training, and it is possible that they also went to Saddleback, but of this I have no specific information.

Great and sudden changes did begin to occur in message content, presentation, Sunday school, number and length of services, and church music.

The first Sunday the new pastor preached, he appeared on stage with slacks, a sport shirt, and coat. But as an omen of things to come, he took his coat off and he appeared to me to be in jogging clothes. Then the choir came in dressed like Rick Warren; then thirty-five deacons came in dressed like Rick Warren; then thirty staff members came in dressed like Rick Warren. The reaction from the membership could be compared to a cold winter wind. Then, because of all the changes, there seemed to be general confusion. No one seemed to know what was going on. Some of the membership began to leave. I began to research Dr. Warren's books, his ministry, and the expanding outreach of the purpose driven church movement. I presented the essence of my research in our March 2004 *Prophetic Observer* as follows:

Piggyback/Saddleback:
Who Is Driving the Purpose Driven Church?

This article is not directed to Saddleback Valley Community Church or its pastor, Rick Warren. It is useless to tell a man who is boating a twelve-pound bass that he is using the wrong bait. This article is directed to pastors who may be pressured into converting their traditional service and mission into a purpose driven church program without due consideration.

When I get my prescription medicines filled at my local pharmacy, there is a page of instructions with each one. At the top of this page is a notice concerning why I am to take this particular medicine. Following is a longer paragraph giving me ten to fifteen reasons why I might not want to take this medicine, because in taking care of one's health problem it may cause many other problems.

Quoting Rick Warren:

> To artificially plant a Saddleback clone in a different environment is a formula for failure. Despite my clear warning, some have tried this anyway and then wondered why things didn't work out. . . . Not one of the twenty-five daughter churches we've started is doing ministry exactly like Saddleback. . . . God has a custom ministry for every church. Your church has a unique thumbprint that God has given it.
>
> —*Purpose Driven Church,* R. Warren, pp. 67–68

In spite of this clear warning by the man himself, thousands of churches worldwide are trying to piggyback on Saddleback, like fishermen in Oklahoma who watch a TV sports show from Florida and rush out to buy the same bait that is catching fish in Lake Okeechobee.

One of the problems I have with some of Pastor Warren's pronouncements is that he will make a rigid statement on one page and then modify or qualify it on the next page. Quoting from an article by Berit Kjos entitled "Spirit-Led or Purpose Driven":

> There are some really good things and points that Rick Warren

brings out. But they always seem to be mixed with so many confusing and theologically weak points that you go crazy trying to keep it all straight.

While Pastor Warren warned against applying Saddleback preachments and practices to the local church, he employed marketing agencies resulting in 60,000 pastors worldwide subscribing to his e-mail newsletter, and more than 250,000 pastors and church leaders from over 125 countries attending purpose driven church seminars.

Quoting from Saddleback's purpose driven web page:

There are thousands of Purpose Driven Churches around the world. Here are just a few that have used the principles to transform their churches. Each of these churches have won a Purpose Driven Church Health Award. Purpose Driven encourage church leaders to investigate PD model churches.

While Pastor Warren decries the cloning of Saddleback Church, his church has spread to a worldwide movement. Thousands of churches in almost every denomination have joined. I could probably find at least one hundred churches in Oklahoma City with a purpose driven sign in front. It is rapidly becoming more pervasive and universal than the charismatic movement of the 1970s. Dr. Ralph Elliott, senior pastor of the North Shore Baptist Church in Chicago, wrote:

My own Baptist church had been in a state of very serious numerical decline since the early 1950s. Then out of nowhere came the promised salvation: the "church growth movement." I bought every book and I read every manual on the subject. Now I am more concerned than ever because I believe this movement to be one of the worst distortions of the church that American ingenuity, born of an outworn capitalist mentality, could possible devise.

Pastor Warren says his great grandfather was converted to Christ through the ministry of Charles Spurgeon in England, but Spurgeon warned about changing the Gospel to accommodate changing society:

> The idea of a progressive gospel seems to have fascinated many. To us that notion is a sort of cross-breed between nonsense and blasphemy. After the gospel has been found effectual in the eternal salvation of untold multitudes, it seems rather late in the day to alter it; and, since it is the revelation of the all-wise and unchanging God, it appears somewhat audacious to attempt its improvement. . . .

The Purpose Driven Pastor

Rick Warren has been praised to the third Heaven by such noted churchmen as W. A. Criswell, Jim Henry, Jerry Falwell, Robert Schuller, Adrian Rogers, Jack Hayford, James Draper, and hundreds more from seminaries around the world. Whether he deserves these accolades from his peers may be debated, but without controversy, Rick Warren has an extremely brilliant mind; he is a hard worker; he is an entrepreneur; he is an innovator and motivator; he is a leader. It took a Rick Warren to build Saddleback Church. But not every church, in fact very few churches, has a pastor like this man, and this is another reason why churches should be cautious about trying to become a piggyback/Saddleback.

One of the dangers with strong church leaders is that they forget God's warning that "pride goes before destruction" and begin to believe what others say about them rather than what God has said to them. Even Lucifer could not withstand this kind of temptation.

The Purpose Driven Dress

In my local church I have served on the deacon board. During my fifteen years in the church we have been blessed with good pastors, including our last one, Dr. Mark Hartman, dispensationally pre-mil and pre-trib. Dr. Anthony Jordan, an excellent preacher, filled in as interim until the search committee presented a new pastor for approval. The vote was 1,871 for and 10 against. I was one of the dissenting ten, because the new pastor was called to change church direction to the purpose driven church program. I certainly had nothing against the new pastor, as I knew little about him. Our church was a loving church, a friendly church, a vibrant and growing church with a solid youth outreach. I personally saw no reason to change ministry and mission direction for unproven programs in our middle class area.

Our pastor came with no coat, no tie, sitting informally on a stool. Church and staff and deacons, about fifty, no coats or ties. Our church was not on Waikiki Beach, Huntington Beach, or the slums of Calcutta. I think the majority were confused and puzzled about what was happening.

Purpose Driven Music

Dr. Warren explains the purpose driven church music like so:

> At Saddleback Church we are unapologetically contemporary.
> . . . And right after we made that decision and stopped trying to
> please everybody, Saddleback exploded with growth. . . . We are
> loud. We are really, really loud. . . . We're not gonna turn it down.
> . . . Baby boomers want to feel the music, not just hear it.
> —"Selecting Worship Music" by R. Warren, July 29, 2002

The "baby boomers" to whom Pastor Warren refers are now between the ages of forty-one and fifty-seven. We would wonder if this age group is listening to the wrong music. Pastor Warren states about traditional hymns that are still sung in many churches today:

To insist that all good music came from Europe 200 years ago, there's a name for that—racism. . . . Encourage members to re-arrange and rewrite.

—Warren on church music,
www.sunlandneighborhoodchurch.com

In his chapter on church music Pastor Warren admits that Saddleback has lost hundreds because of their music, but have gained thousands also because of their music. On page 281 of *Purpose Driven Church,* he states further:

There is no such a thing as "Christian music," only Christian lyrics.

When Moses came down from Mount Sinai he heard the noise of the people and knew before he heard their words that they were worshipping the golden calf and engaging in sinful activities (Exod. 32). The same erotic music that accompanied the entertainment during the Super Bowl halftime show is the same type of music that has been brought into the church to worship the Lord.

At my church there were complaints about the music, so Sunday morning worship was divided into two services: traditional service at 9:00 a.m. and contemporary service at 10:30 a.m. The rock-and-roll beat is out of synchronization with our pulse and heartbeat and induces a fight-or-flight response.

Purpose Driven Bibles
In the endnotes to Pastor Warren's book, *The Purpose Driven Life,* I counted the scripture references made in the book. I may have missed a few, but this is what is listed to the best of my knowledge:

NLT	127	NIV	117	TEV	78	MSG	98
LB	66	NCV	56	GWT	26	CEV	48

| NASB | 6 | KJV | 13 | NRSV | 5 | AMP | 4 |
| JB | 1 | NJB | 3 | PH | 6 | | |

Only the King James Version is a translation of literal equivalency from the Received Text. The other fourteen Bibles from which Pastor Warren quoted scripture are based on the Westcott and Hort text, which used the corrupted Alexandrian text, which has been further corrupted by liberal scholarship using dynamic equivalency and paraphrasing. Some have accused Pastor Warren of searching the newer expanded translations until he finds a scripture that more nearly agrees with what he wants it to say rather than simply applying the Word of God, and this is why he uses so many newer versions.

While Pastor Warren seems deeply concerned about racism in the hymns Christians have sung for the past two or three hundred years, he seems unconcerned about the Westcott and Hort text Bibles from which he quotes. Westcott and Hort were rabid racists and violently anti-American. Professor John Anthony Hort of Cambridge stated without qualifications:

> I hate it [slavery] much more for its influence on the whites than on the niggers themselves. . . . Everywhere they have surely shown themselves as an immeasurably inferior race, just human and no more; . . . their highest virtues those of a good Newfoundland dog. . . . I care more for England . . . than all the niggers in the world. . . . The American empire is a standing menace to the whole civilization of Europe. . . . It cannot be wrong to desire and pray from the bottom of one's heart that the American union be shivered to pieces.
>
> —from *Letters of John Anthony Hort,*
> Vol. 2, p. 458, published by his son

One of the newer paraphrased versions that Pastor Rick seems to favor is *The Message.* The main objection to this so-called version is that the word "Bible" is on the cover. It reads like the vernacular of a high school dropout or a joke book about the Bible. Some of the chapters, like from the Song of Solomon, would be embarrassing to read in mixed company. When writing this, I opened *The Message* and let it open by itself and read,

> It is obvious what kind of life develops out of trying to get your own way all the time: repetitive, loveless, cheap sex, a stinking accumulation of mental and emotional garbage . . . impotence to love. . . .

We wonder what the next newer version will be like.

The Purpose Driven Dollar

When we think of CNN we do not confine our image to just one building in Atlanta. CNN reaches around the world. The same is true of Saddleback Church and Pastor Warren. According to published reports, sixty thousand pastors around the world subscribe to his e-mail newsletter. Thousands daily order his sermons at four dollars each. Tens of thousands attend Pastor Warren's seminars, and his Internet program goes around the world. His first book, *The Purpose Driven Church,* has sold more than one million copies, and we quote from a publication news magazine by Pastor Warren's publisher, Zondervan:

> It's fair to call the popularity of *The Purpose Driven Life* by Rick Warren epidemic. The book released in October of 2002 and debuted at number two on the Christian bookstore bestseller list in the first month it was eligible. By the next month it had risen to the top where it remains to this day. But the popularity of this book is not limited to the traditional Christian audience. Its sales increased through all manner of stores until it appeared on the *New York Times* bestseller's list, eventually reaching number one. Barely a year old, the book has sold more than five million copies and outsold every

other book in the United States except Harry Potter, dominating every retail channel and bestseller list along the way.

I knew Pat Zondervan. Zondervan published one of my books in the 1960s. After Pat was called home to be with the Lord, the company was sold to Rupert Murdoch, reported to be the richest man in the world. The gross sales on Pastor Warren's latest book alone is expected to gross more than $500 million. In almost every Christian bookstore in this nation, as well as many secular bookstores here and abroad, Pastor Warren's books are prominently displayed. Marketing agencies, and PR and advertising firms, are busy promoting the Saddleback ministries in their various procedures and outreach. When this happens with dozens of contracts involved, the genesis personality loses control. The dollar becomes the main ministry motivation rather than the Gospel. I wonder today how much control Pastor Warren has over the purpose driven church movement.

Purpose Driven Prophecy

While writing this article, on February 7, 2004, I checked once more the Saddleback web and copied an article by Pastor Warren titled "Becoming a Purpose Driven Church—Vision & Strategy":

> The greatest challenge churches will face over the next five years is developing and adapting our ministry methods to the massive needs of the 21st century. We can't just keep on "doing it the way we've always done it." . . . We must start thousands of new churches and services. It will take new churches to reach a new generation. . . . We must develop a clear, practical strategy. . . . If we don't, thousands of churches are going to close up for good. This doesn't have to happen. . . . Thousands of pastors and church leaders have attended the Purpose Driven Church seminars. . . . The secret of reaching unbelievers is learning to think like an un-

believer. The problem is, the longer you're a Christian, the less you think like an unbeliever. You have to intentionally learn to think like an unbeliever again . . . such as changing the way you greet visitors, the style of music that you use, the translation you preach from. . . .

—*www.pastors.com/RWMT/?id=50&artid=778&expand=1*

Maybe I missed something, but we read in Romans 8:6, "to be carnally minded is death," and we read that a double-minded man is unstable in all his ways. We are told repeatedly in the Bible to "put on the mind of Christ," not the mind of the world. The mindset of the world is why the world is in the mess it is in. The Word of God tells us expressly that you cannot solve a sinners' problem until he or she first seeks the Kingdom of God—born again by faith in Jesus Christ. Are we now to believe that we first have to change sinners' circumstances and somewhere down the road they will be saved? This has been tried before; I believe we called them "rice Christians."

Pastor Warren started out by warning churches not to clone Saddleback, but now he seems to be telling all the churches, worldwide, that unless they become Saddleback clones they won't be around in five years.

Winds of spiritual change have blown through the church many times, the latest being Promise Keepers. Some have left a breath of fresh air and some a pungent smog. The purpose driven church movement like the others will pass, and in due course Jesus Christ will come for His church (1 Thess. 4:13–18).

Purpose Driven Gospel

One thing that confuses me about the pulpit preaching of Pastor Warren is, does the hear-no-evil and see-no-evil message bring the sinner under conviction to know that he or she is lost so that they can be saved? The CBMC newsletter of December 22, 2003, carried a message by Rick Warren. We quote Pastor Warren's understanding of being saved:

> ... What we need most is salvation—so God sent us a Saviour. What is "salvation"? It's forgiveness for my past, ... power to manage my present problems, ... and a guarantee for my future.

Power to manage problems is the result of salvation, not a part of it. While this message may change lost sinners into better lost sinners through "churchanity" osmosis, it is not the Gospel which is the power of God unto salvation to everyone who receives Jesus Christ as Saviour and Lord. We would hope that CBMC either misquoted Pastor Warren or left something out.

Purpose Driven Departures

The Fundamental Evangelistic Association of Los Osos, California, quotes Pastor Warren on their website (*www.fundamentalbiblechurch. org*) as advising churches who adapt the purpose driven church program:

> Be willing to let people leave the church. And I told you earlier the fact that people are gonna leave the church no matter what you do. But when you define the vision, you're choosing who leaves. You say, "But Rick, yes, they're the pillars of the church." Now, you know what pillars are. Pillars are people who hold things up. . . . And in your church, you may have to have some blessed subtractions before you have any real additions.

At my church we have had some "blessed subtractions," and until the "real additions" show up I am enjoying just driving up within a few feet of the church rather than having to walk two or three blocks from outside parking lots.

There are many other comments and concerns about this Rupert Rip-Off we could address, space permitting. I close with a final word of advice to pastors considering taking the plunge:

1. Have your home mortgage paid up,
2. Have some extra food in the freezer, and
3. Start praying about your next pastorate.

. . . . .

Our announcer, Jerry Guiltner, sent a copy of this *Prophetic Observer* to a couple of his friends and received the following reply:

Your mail came today with the "Brother Hutchings" *Prophetic Observer* on the Saddleback church growth movement! I cannot express adequately my excitement after reading it! It is like an answer to prayer and you two were the angels who delivered it to us! Thank you ever so much. I will use this over and over again as I try my best to convince others that our churches are under a siege to secularize the very spiritual foundation that undergirds its biblical purpose.

It took only the first few lines for me to recognize it as an objective evaluation, and then authentic by its source references and undergirded with verifiable examples. This is not the rambling rantings of some prejudiced rebel. I have tried many times to figure out exactly how to describe the spiritual conflicts of Rick Warren's concepts. This article does it so very well.

Can you tell me anything about Dr. N. W. Hutchings? We are going to search the Web to see if we can find him there.

I am going to send a copy of this to Becky and Steve there in Oklahoma City. Dr. Hutchings was apparently speaking of --------- [his former] Church where they were attending and are now looking elsewhere. I remember her describing the introduction by the new pastor of informality in structure and clothing.

I have an appointment with the pastor of County Acres Baptist Church on August 10 and am going to make a copy of this available to him.

Thank you ever so much.

Not only did everyone on our current mailing list get a copy, but we began to get orders for hundreds and thousands. Subsequently, I began to get letters from church members across the nation and even abroad. David Wilkerson of World Challenge, Inc. wrote me the following letter on June 21, 2004:

Dear Dr. Hutchings:

Your article concerning Rick Warren's ministry is one of the most balanced exposés of what I see as a very dangerous movement. I find no animosity in what you have said and I believe it is a message that every pastor around the world needs to hear.

As I've traveled the world the last two years in ministers' conferences, I've seen the havoc which that ministry has caused. In South Africa, one pastor spent six weeks preaching from Rick Warren's book. Most of his well-grounded pillars left the church and it is floundering. We find the same everywhere we go. It simply does not work.

I've ordered one hundred copies of "Piggyback/Saddleback" and plan to send them to my bishop friends in all the nations we've been to.

God bless you for taking the stand that is not popular and one that I believe truly pleases the Lord.

May the Spirit of the Lord give you strength and courage. Well said, my brother.

His bondservant,
David Wilkerson

From my own conclusions drawn from what I had observed at my church, and from the serious concerns expressed in letters, telephone calls, and e-mails from disturbed church members across the nations, there is another side to the purpose driven church movement—a dark side.

Chapter 3

Getting Rid
of the
Old Church Pillars

Dr. Warren in building Saddleback Church, according to his own account, sent out letters to those residents in the area containing a questionnaire about what kind of church they would attend if such a church was located near them. The letter was directed to the churched and unchurched alike. The larger percentage of the unchurched would also be non-Christians, or whom I would call the unsaved. But to maintain standard Christian interpretations or meanings would limit attendance, so definitions had to change: not the saved and unsaved, but the churched and unchurched. Subsequently, even denominational titles have been removed and some purpose driven churches are simply known as campuses.

Dr. Warren is reported as advising, if there is opposition to change within the membership, then get rid of the old pillars, because old pillars are only good for holding things up. The new pastor at my church evidently took Dr. Warren at his word. The older Sunday school classes seemed to have been moved to the back of the educational buildings; music and church functions for the teenagers and members below fifty was promoted and financed. Many of the older members began leaving even before I did. I was not used to sermons about the Power Rangers and Teenage Mutant Ninja Turtles or having the senior church members who had worked, served, and given to build up the church from a mission to the number two Baptist church of our state treated like second-class, third-class, or fourth-class church members. Also, after four months of the new pastor and church administration, the membership was still in the dark about where the church was going. On or about March 10, 2004, I sent the following letter to the president of our senior Sunday school department:

Dear Charles:

This letter is to advise you and the class that I will no longer be attending the senior class under your supervision. Kim will be making her own decision, but as far as I know, she will leave with me.

This has nothing to do with anything you or anyone else in class has done or said. We have nothing but love and respect for you, Richard, and the rest of the class. We have been blessed of the Lord to have been members of --------- for the past fifteen years.

Frankly, I have had some concerns about the process in which the new pastor was chosen. I also have some concerns over the new mission and message of the church in the change to a purpose driven church program. I also have other concerns about the leadership, whomever that may be, not fully informing the church body about specific details of the change. I feel that the majority of the attending membership still has no idea about what the new program is all about. In any event, I feel --------- will not be the same church I joined or have attended.

Inasmuch as my reservations about the new course the church is taking will prevent my unqualified support, rather than being a negative influence, it is best that we look for another church home.

Regardless of my concerns, we will pray for the success of the church in its Church Growth outreach and that many souls will be saved.

Faithfully yours,
Noah W. Hutchings

From the time I posted this letter, I never received another piece of mail from the church, even though I did not change my church membership or church letter until three months later, and even though some members of my family had not been to the church for five years, they continued to get church materials. No one from the Sunday school department called to tell me they would miss me, or to kiss their feet, or to kiss any other part of their anatomy. No one from the church office called to thank me for my years of faithful service, for serving on the deacon board, or for helping in raising $2½ million dollars on the new youth building. No, sir, they were glad to get rid of this old pillar who had some concerns about the purpose driven church program. Cults cannot stand opposition, or even discussion, much less questions. This is the way the new purpose driven leadership thinks. This is the way your former Christian friends have been brainwashed. You are suddenly their enemy!

While the purpose driven church program can come into a traditional church with an ongoing pastor, the process is much easier to install when the search committee is looking for a PDC man during a pastoral change. This is what happened at my former church, and I have received many letters, calls, and e-mails where this has happened across the nation. Church members need to be extremely cautious in accepting a new pastor simply upon the recommendation of a few deacons, staff members, or the so-called "search" committee. An example of the letters I have received when this happened came from Mr. & Mrs. B. & P. of Tabernacle, New Jersey:

Dear Noah:

Our story begins with a young, promising pastor of our former church. Nevertheless, he was called with a 97 percent vote to the Baptist (GARB) church of which we were members and serving in. Aside from being misrepresented by the search committee, and the church conditioned to a one man rule philosophy, this man was set up with unquestioned authority to impose his purpose driven program on this church of about 350 attendees and members.

We did not know much about Rev. Rick Warren at the time, but noticed a trend toward non-traditional type programs and music. The choir was cut in half by authoritarian manipulation. It became obvious he didn't want much of a choir anyway except for bit parts in congregational music as a worship team would do.

This pastor had the unabashed audacity to offend and shun long-term members. In effect, he booted them out the door, as most who left were never called or visited by him or his puppet deacon board. Many dedicated and gifted servants of the Lord were rudely abused and displaced from their ministry posts.

This purpose driven leader is now in his fourth year of non-ministry. The facility of twenty years is beautiful, paid for (before he came) and seats about 600–700 people. The good things still going on were established long before he came on the scene. Many are in serious jeopardy and others have ceased. The church is debt-free, has $300,000 in CDs, a "yes man" deacon board (his hand-picked staff to do his bidding), and allows the unchallenged manipulating of funds. He ignores and abuses established members and caters to "his" new members, all the while preaching that "people matter." Sounds like a facility takeover plan to me.

While we endured these atrocities for three years, we became aware of two sizeable sister churches (GARB) within a fifteen mile radius, which were also steeped in purpose driven programs and who had similar horror stories. A charter member of one of those churches received a letter stating that their membership would be terminated because they questioned the pastor's practices and challenged him in a business meeting. They left first before they were terminated. The secretary of the other church was fired because she didn't "get on board" with the purpose driven programs there.

My wife and I left about a year ago. I gave the pastor a copy of your newsletter and related materials that put Rick Warren in a bad light. I understand now he doesn't mention purpose driven as much, but his destructive patterns continue. We now attend a Missionary Alliance Church of 2,200 and three services. It is very contemporary but good preaching and excellent outreach. My wife is an excellent pianist and organist and we were both choir members for thirty-five years—all our married life. We haven't really seen the need to get involved since they have no organ and use mostly keyboard as they have a lot of established talent. We feel somewhat displaced.

Thanks for your faithful ministry at SWRC. We have been listening for thirty-seven years and support you as we are able.

Thank you for reading this letter. If you can use any of the content in your proposed book, please do so. We are some of the victims of the purpose driven church. There may be some good things in Mr. Warren's materials, but it has deprived us of our ministries at this time in our lives. We take comfort in the Blessed Hope.

"Even so, come Lord Jesus."

Although I do not remember the exact number on the church roll of my former church, I would estimate it would have been approximately five thousand. The church, when I left, was debt-free and $2½ million had been raised for a new youth building that was to be erected. This building was completed after I left.

During the fifteen months after I left, and at the writing of this book, the mass exodus from the church because of the purpose driven church program has continued. Each Sunday morning as I drive by going to my present church, there appear to be fewer cars in the parking lot. Many have gone to Village Baptist Church; Quail Springs Baptist Church; Cherokee Hills Baptist Church; First Baptist Church of Bethany; and other Baptist or independent churches. Those with whom I have talked who have left for other churches tell me they always call before visiting a church to find out if the church is a PDC church, or plans on using PDC programs like the forty days of purpose. If so, then they will look for another church to visit. A friend who continued to attend my former church told me that most of the church staff had been dismissed. I also heard from a former member that the church had been mortgaged to pay salaries. Another reported to me that at the last Sunday morning service the attendance was so small that everyone could be seated in one section of the auditorium.

It is not easy for seniors who have supported, prayed, and ministered in a church for years to be suddenly subjected to abrupt, abrasive changes and have to search for another place to worship. Some with whom I have talked who have left my former church have actually cried, and not so much for their own loss, but the loss of a beautiful and community-serving church.

When Dr. Warren speaks on CNN, writes for national magazines, and millions of his books are sold to awestruck readers, you will not hear about stories like this or the one in the letter from the couple in New Jersey. It has been reported that Dr. Warren has stated that he takes no blame for negative actions within the purpose driven church movement or individual churches. If the buck doesn't stop with Dr. Warren, where does it stop?

Change Agents

One of the agencies that Dr. Warren and the purpose driven church movement uses to change a church from its traditional model, which I consider a New Testament model, to a contemporary or purpose driven model, is *Church Transitions* of Fort Lauderdale, Florida (*www.*

churchtransitions.com). According to information on the organization's web site, they have trained one hundred thousand church leaders and "about half of the events . . . are co-sponsored by Purpose Driven Ministries." Also, according to the web site, the training is based on the book of Nehemiah. It is interesting that the purpose driven church program is based on a book from the Old Testament instead of Acts, Ephesians, or the pastoral epistles. But since it is obvious that Dr. Warren is a replacement theologian, why not?

The reason that the large percentage of letters we have received from hundreds of church members who have left their churches because they went purpose driven follow the same pattern is because church leaders who go the PDC route get the same training. From the manual they are told that if they follow instructions and do A-B-C-D-E-F-G-H, their church will grow to a mega-church just like Saddleback, or if it is not said in so many words, it is at least implied. This vision has tens of thousands of would-be Warrens frothing at the mouth, already lining up to be interviewed by Larry King on CNN.

The Church Transitions organization list eight steps that pastors and church staff members will be trained to follow in changing their churches from a traditional church to a purpose driven church. The eight steps as listed are:

The process of transition that we teach is a simple one:

Step one—Prepare for change

Step two—Define your changes

Step three—Plant your vision with your key leaders

Step four—Share your vision with the whole church

Step five—Implement your changes

Step six—Deal with the opposition

Step seven—Make adjustments

Step eight—Evaluate the result

It will be noted by the reader that in my letter to my former church, I charged that the membership was not being told what was happening, and this is the same story in hundreds of letters we have received from almost every state. The reason is that the pastor and staff members promoting the program are instructed by Dr. Warren not to say anything until the fourth step. This is why Dr. Warren says:

> Be willing to let people leave the church. And I told you earlier the fact that people are gonna leave the church no matter what you do. But when you define the vision, you're choosing who leaves. You say, "But Rick, yes, they're the pillars of the church." Now, you know what pillars are. Pillars are people who hold things up. . . . And in your church, you may have to have some blessed subtractions before you have real additions.

The problem is that in far too many cases the "old pillars" leaving far outnumber any additions, and it is the "old pillars" who pay the pastor's and staff's salaries, the utilities, and the church mortgage.

Also, many of the letters, e-mails, and calls we have received note a common complaint: "We didn't know this was happening until it happened. What can we do about it?"

Of course the membership usually doesn't know anything about the transition until it is already done. They don't know because they are not supposed to know. The PDC advocates have already stolen the church, and once this has happened, there is very little if anything the membership can do except look for another church home. The letter below from a listener in Pampa, Texas, is just one of hundreds:

Pastor Hutchings:

Thank you for sending me a copy of your newsletter. For the past thirty-five years our family has been part of a Bible church here in Pampa.

Three years ago we hired a pastor from Illinois with nine years experience. Three adult children and a lovely helpful wife. He was well received and well liked. Two years ago he attended a pastors' conference in California. Then the changes began and an emphasis on reaching the unchurched. As a board member and founder of the church, several of us tried to get our pastor to lay out his agenda and why he was changing the direction and purpose of our church. He denies he has an agenda but many of his ideas for change are right out of *The Purpose Driven Church*.

Four of the board members and their families have left the church along with many others.

So what you described in your newsletter has happened in two or more of the churches in Pampa. Friends in Lubbock have experienced the same thing.

Best regards.

The pastor probably attended a transition church seminar sponsored by Saddleback or Church Transitions, and probably at his church's expense. And this is another dark side of the purpose driven church movement that is not exposed to the light in Dr. Warren's books, web site, or preachments.

Chapter 4

Forty Days to Nowhere

The first book by Dr. Warren, *The Purpose Driven Church,* sold over a million copies according to the publisher's note on the cover of his second book, *The Purpose Driven Life.* While there are no current figures available, as far as I know, as to the dissemination of his second book, our estimate would be over thirty million as the number sold was reported over twenty million in 2004.

The questions which Dr. Warren proposed to answer in *The Purpose Driven Life*—Who Am I? Why am I here? And where am I going?—are those used by hundreds or thousands of preachers and authors of Christian books to lay a base for a message or dissertation. The difference in Dr. Warren's book, where the questions are presented, is that he proposed to give the reader the answer in forty days. Once the reader, or Christian as the case may be, gets the answers, then he or she will be a fully matured disciple ready and willing for fruitful service, according to Rick Warren.

Dr. Warren writes in the introduction to *The Purpose Driven Life:* "The Bible is clear that God considers 40 days a spiritually significant time period. Whenever God wanted to prepare someone for his purposes, he took 40 days."

Dr. Warren continues to give eight examples:

1. **"Noah's life was transformed by 40 days of rain."** Really? Noah had already been a preacher of righteousness for 120 years. To build a huge boat when it had never rained must have already taken more faith than we can possibly imagine (2 Pet. 2:5). There is no evidence that the forty days of rain transformed Noah, because he did not need to be transformed. What the forty days of rain did do was to kill everyone in the world except eight souls on the ark.

2. **"Moses was transformed by 40 days on Mount Sinai."** There is no evidence that Moses was transformed from anything or to anything on Mount Sinai while receiving the Law from God. Forty is a biblical number of judgment or probation, and by the "law shall no flesh be justified" (Gal. 2:16). Moses' impatient nature, which got him into trouble several times, was manifested again when he came down from Mount Sinai after the forty days (Exod. 32:19).

3. **"The spies were transformed by 40 days in the Promised Land."** Really? We read in Numbers 12 that twelve spies went to spy out the Promised Land. Ten went into the Promised Land cowards and came out cowards. Two went in brave men and came out brave men. Forty days didn't change a single one. As a result, Israel wandered in the wilderness for forty years until that generation perished.

We will not consider the other five examples presented by Dr. Warren of spiritual transformation, but you get the idea.

To me, and also noted by others, this book that has sold some thirty million copies is based at the beginning on a false premise. If Dr. Warren wanted to attach his "vision" to biblical numerics, why not use the number seven or the multiple of seven, forty-nine? Forty, throughout Scripture, is the number of judgment, testing, or failure. All men born of Adam die. It was after four thousand years a second Adam came to deliver lost mankind from the curse of the first Adam. Four thousand is one hundred times forty. The common date that most chronologists agree for the Olivet Discourse where Jesus prophesied the destruction of Jerusalem and the temple is A.D. 30. Forty years later, in A.D. 70, this judgment came because Israel as a nation continued to reject Jesus Christ as the rightful heir to the throne of David.

The Lord may have told Noah to go out and build an ark, but He has not told this Noah to do that. The Lord may have told Moses to go up on top of Mount Sinai for forty days and forty nights, but He has not told me to do that. What the Lord has told me to do as a Christian is found in the epistles to the churches, and nowhere can I find that God has told me to sit on a mountain, wander the Promised Land, or pat my tummy and rub my head for forty days, or any other numbers of days. Particularly absent also in the epistles is to spend forty days reading and studying *The Purpose Driven Life*.

In the Old Testament where the Kingdom promise is presented, everything was numbered: the gold was counted, the silver was counted, the tribes were counted, the cattle was counted, and even the concubines, wives, and servants, were counted, as well as those who fell in battle. In the four Gospels, numbering continued because Jesus Christ came to offer the Kingdom to Israel: the apostles were numbered (twelve); the seventy disciples sent out were numbered; the five thousand who were fed were numbered; the number of loaves and fishes were numbered, and even the 153 fish caught in a net were numbered. In the first few chapters of Acts, the Kingdom continued to be offered to Israel on a conditional basis that Israel repent of killing their Messiah and pray for God to send Jesus Christ back: "Repent ye therefore, and be converted, that your sins may be blotted out, when the times of refreshing shall come from the presence of the Lord; And he shall send Jesus Christ, which before was preached unto you" (Acts 3:19–20).

During this brief period of the all-Jewish church, numbering was approximate: *about* three thousand added to the one hundred twenty disciples; and to this number was added *about* five thousand more (Acts 2:41; 4:4). After Acts 4, practically all numbering in reference to the church ceased. Nowhere do we read after this where additions to the church, or church membership, was numbered. We are in the gap between the sixty-ninth and seventieth prophetic weeks of Daniel when God is calling out of the gentile nations a people for His Name, the church (Acts 15). When we get to Revelation, when we believe (although some disagree) the church will be taken out of the world before the Tribulation begins, numbering appears again: seven angels, seven scrolls, seven vials, seven trumpets, seven thunders, 144,000, 200 million, two witnesses, twelve tribes of Israel, etc.

Numbering is absent in the church because only God knows whom on the church rolls is truly saved. In fact, observing of days is forbidden (Col. 2:16). This is also indicated in Galatians 4:9-11:

> But now, after that ye have known God, or rather are known of God, how turn ye again to the weak and beggarly elements, whereunto ye desire again to be in bondage? Ye observe days, and months, and times, and years. **I am afraid of you, lest I have bestowed upon you labour in vain** (Emphasis mine).

Becoming more like Jesus Christ in our relationship to our family, friends, neighbors, and fellow employees, is not a time-oriented process limited to days. It is a continuing spiritual experience (2 Pet. 1:2–11).

It is not my intention to take the reader on a forty-day, 334-page trip through Dr. Warren's book to nowhere. Others have done that already. For those who would prefer a page-by-page detailed study of the Warren gospel, I suggest, *Who's Driving the Purpose Driven Church?* by James Sundquist, published by Bible Belt Publishing.

In a web site article by Richard Abanes, author of *Rick Warren and the Purpose That Drives Him*, Abanes deals with Dr. Warren's critics. He states that fundamentalists are the harshest because they make "Warren look as bad as possible." Abanes complains:

> It must be remembered that Warren is not a professional author. He is a pastor. And his writing must be read in light of his preaching and doctrinal positions. Neither of these additional sources of information, however, are being regularly consulted by critics. Indeed, his many sermons/lectures have been virtually ignored. . . .
>
> —*www.abanes.com/warrencritics.html*

Now, if Dr. Warren cannot really say what he means all the time, how are we to know when he really means what he says. And if the reader of his two principal books have to go back and read his messages over the past twenty years to get what he means, why buy the books in the first place? If thirty million readers of his books cannot know what they are reading, they must think they know what they are reading, or else they have been totally hoodwinked.

In this, I am reminded of the story about the emperor who had been convinced that he was wearing the finest suit of clothes ever designed and tailored by man. He believed it so strongly that all his subjects in the kingdom dared not disagree with him, and swooned in admiration as he passed by. Finally, a young lad who had not been told the king had no clothes on, ran out of the crowd laughing and pointing his finger, yelling, "Hey, this old guy is as naked as a newly hatched jay bird."

The truth often hurts, and it is amazing and almost unthinkable that one hundred thousand pastors, or more, have fallen for this purpose driven bad-news message.

> Because thou sayest, I am rich, and increased with goods, and have need of nothing; and knowest not that thou art wretched, and

miserable, and poor, and blind, *and naked:* I counsel thee to buy of me gold tried in the fire, that thou mayest be rich; and white raiment, that thou mayest be clothed, and that the *shame* of thy *nakedness* do not appear; and anoint thine eyes with eyesalve, that thou mayest see.

—Revelation 3:17–18

On page 99 of his book, Abanes practically flushes Dr. Bob Schuller down the toilet in order to distance him from Dr. Warren. Yet, if Rick Warren's name was not on the article "Learn to Love Yourself" in the March 2005 *Ladies Home Journal* (p. 36), we would think it was written by Dr. Schuller. To paraphrase Shakespeare, a skunk by any other name would smell just as bad. This article is about loving yourself to wonderland and God will receive you. This is an article that will be read by millions who have never read the first verse in the Bible, who have never entered a church, who are walking and living in spiritual darkness, who are on their way to Hell. Yet, Dr. Warren does not even reference one scripture, but concludes this naked narcissistic message with:

You can believe what others say about you, or you can believe in yourself as does God, who says you are truly acceptable, lovable, valuable, and capable.

What does the Bible say?

But we are all as an unclean thing, and all our righteousnesses are as filthy rags. . . .

—Isaiah 64:6

As it is written, There is none righteous, no, not one: There is none that understandeth, there is none that seeketh after God.

—Romans 3:10–11

We give thanks to God and the Father of our Lord Jesus Christ
. . . Who hath delivered us from the power of darkness, and hath
translated us into the kingdom of his dear Son: In whom we have
redemption through his blood, even the forgiveness of sins.

—Colossians 1:3,13–14

Loving yourself will not get you accepted by God. By faith going to the
cross with Jesus Christ who died for you sins, will. Any other message
will get those who are deceived the darkness of Hell forever.

Chapter 5

What Is the Message in
The Message?

There are now over three hundred versions of the Bible that have appeared since 1881 when Drs. Westcott and Hort took the Alexandrian texts and produced a new Greek New Testament. One of the latest, if not the latest, is *The Message* (The Bible in Contemporary Language), or in contemptible language, depending upon the point of view. *The Message* is becoming the holy book, or "holey" book, of the purpose driven church movement. Dr. Rick Warren references *The Message* ninety-eight times in his book *The Purpose Driven Life*, and it is referenced a majority over other newer translations in a new capsule-sized edition of *The Purpose Driven Life* titled *What on Earth Am I Here For?*, just published by Rupert Murdoch through Zondervan Publishing.

Rupert Murdoch, who owns and/or controls dozens of publishing and media concerns, has showcased Dr. Warren in almost every metropolis and hamlet in over two hundred nations. The more popular that Dr. Warren and the PDC become, the more money Rupert makes, and the more money Rupert makes, the more money Dr. Warren has to spread the "saving" message of the new contemporary gospel. Without Rupert, Dr. Warren would probably be a modestly successful, liberal, social gospel pastor in a local Saddleback setting.

Dr. Theodore Letis, author of *The Ecclesiastical Text*, and professor at Concordia University, summed up his opinion of the PDC thusly:

He decided he wanted to be a winner instead of a loser, and so in a Mephistopheles manner, he suddenly became successful —the way all mega-churches become successful—by appealing to the American middle class angst with the salve of affirmation. He has taken Wayne Dyer's pop-psychology/New Age hippie cosmology (see Dyer's book and VERY popular PBS video/DVD TV series: **Power of Intention: Learning to Co-Create Your World Your Way**), given it a dumbed-down, evangelical spin, and like Dyer (an academic drop-out from the field of philosophy), he has become a very successful—and I suspect—a very wealthy man.

[Warren] has gutted the Christian faith of all its content, thus maximizing his capacity to appeal to ALL religious backgrounds, as well as the "unchurched" who possess sizable incomes, but sadly, with no place to direct it. He has learned what has driven the corporate world in the United States for years: make people feel good, and they will keep coming back for strokes (i.e., your product). The entire project is superbly endemic to American middle-class religious folk who want religion to make them feel good about themselves, without traditional religious trappings. It is nothing more, nor anything less, than American corporate-world, motivational seminar religion. It is the perfect formula for success, which is what rather pathetic Mr. Warren was after all along.

Look—no pastor wants to be a loser—hence, this Warren success stuff is going to appeal to a certain kind of pastor. Those with their nose in Scripture, Church history, and theology will see this for what it is. The other kind of pastor—and you KNOW who you are—will be on board in a heartbeat.

Always keep in mind that the early believers gave their lives for religious language—*homoousios,* rather than *homoiousios.* "Of" the same essence versus "like" the same essence (Christ being one with the Father as God).

ANYONE who wants to gut the Christian faith of her vocabulary for the sake of Church growth, is *not* a shepherd but a cheap hireling. . . .

There you are, my good friends, again, my unvarnished, unsugarcoated telling of the truth, a rarer and rarer phenomenon in the world today.

Dr. Letis was taken to his heavenly reward in June 2005 in an unfortunate automobile accident. So those who wish to rebuke him for his rather abrasive terminology will have to contact him at his new address.

In chapter two I presented the seven principal aspects of the PDC movement, and the one that I will try to enlarge upon in this commentary is the purpose driven Bibles. To me, this is the most obvious concern related to the PDC movement. In order to replace the New Testament type church with a new PDC contemporary operation, everything related to service and worship must be replaced. The music, dress, Sunday school, assembly times, number of assemblies, décor, seating, and even the room assignments, must change. Not every church that does the PDL "40 Days in the Wilderness" program advances to a full PDC format, but the most adaptable switch for PDL disciples is to change their Bibles.

It is not my intention in this book to aggressively defend my preference for the Textus Receptus and KJV. Those who prefer one of the newer versions based on the 1881 Greek New Testament by Westcott and Hort, which is from the Sinaiticus and Vaticanus (Catholic texts), should please consider that you and I have a difference of opinion. As far as the KJV is concerned, if it was good enough for Washington, Jefferson, and Lincoln, then it's good enough for me.

In *The Purpose Driven Life*, which by now has sold over thirty million copies (and added a few more million bucks to Rupert Murdoch's bank account), Dr. Warren references fifteen versions of the Bible, with *The Message* being one of the favorites (ninety-eight references). In the latest PDL booklet, *The Message* is referenced more than any of the new versions. Dr. Warren has advised PDC advocates to switch to new versions, and it is obvious that *The Message* is becoming the "word" of the purpose driven church. Other than Bill McCartney, founder and president of Promise Keepers, and Bill Hybels, pastor of Willow Creek, only a few nominal ecclesiastics and unknown entertainers dared to endorse it. However, not so with Dr. Rick Warren. With Dr. Warren recommending *The Message* through his books to seventy thousand pastors and thirty million-plus church members, *The Message* is rapidly winning the popularity polls with the seekers and suckers alike.

The storyteller of *The Message*, Dr. Eugene H. Peterson, obviously used the Alexandrian texts instead of the Received Text as a base for his latest essay about what he believes about God and His message. We can know this from 1 John 4:1–3 alone. And, according to the questionable endorsements, "*The Message* is the easiest of all the new translations to understand; it is the most accurate; it captures the real meaning of the original messages of the writers of the Old and New Testaments." John 1:1 is a biblical test verse for a translations' accuracy and credibility:

In the beginning was the Word and the Word was with God, and the Word was God.

There are no verse numbers in *The Message*, on purpose, so it will be more difficult to check and compare scripture. But the first five lines in *The Message* on John were comparative, so I read:

The Word was first, the Word present to God, God present to the Word, The Word was God, in readiness for God from day one.

Will someone please write and tell me what this means? It is evident that Dr. Peterson didn't know what it meant.

Next, I wondered what *The Message* had done to such passages as the beatitudes, so I read first from Matthew 5:

v. 5 Blessed are the meek: for they shall inherit the earth.

v. 6 Blessed are they which do hunger and thirst after righteousness: for they shall be filled. . . .

v. 8 Blessed are the pure in heart: for they shall see God.

Next, I turned to the seemingly comparative paraphrases in *The Message* and read:

v. 5 You're blessed when you're content with just who you are—no more, no less. That's the moment you find yourselves proud owners of everything that can't be bought.

v. 6 You're blessed when you've worked up a good appetite for God. He's food and drink in the best meal you'll ever eat. . . .

v. 8 You're blessed when you get your inside world—your mind and heart—put right. Then you can see God in the outside world.

Other than endorsing narcissism and pantheism, I get no meaning from Dr. Peterson's interpretation of the Sermon on the Mount. Otherwise, I must appropriate these paraphrase meanderings to the mouthing of an inebriated priest who has lingered a little too long at the Benedictine bottle.

It is one thing to dumb down church members with vernacular translations, but quite another to make Jesus Christ sound like the village idiot, saying things that He never said. I personally would not want to answer at the Judgment Seat for editing or rewriting what Jesus said. I, for one, think Jesus knew what He wanted to say, and said it.

Dr. Eugene Peterson, as reported in *Christianity Today* (December 23, 2002), stated when asked if he considered *The Message* God's Word:

> ...in a congregation where somebody uses it in the Scripture reading, it makes me uneasy.

> I would never recommend it to be used as, "hear the Word of God from the Message." It surprises me how many do.

> I like to hear those more formal languages in the pulpit.

> I did the Beatitudes in about 10 minutes.

We respect Dr. Peterson for saying that he does not use his own contemporary paraphrase; that it should not be considered the Word of God; and that it should not be used in formal worship service. Yet Dr. Rick Warren and thousands of others will quote from *The Message* and say, "God says here..."

In the third chapter of Ephesians, Paul references the mystery of the church that Jesus Christ gave to him by revelation, but near the end of the chapter *The Message* adds these words to those of the apostle, "And so here I am, preaching and writing about things that are way over my head...." In my brief study of *The Message* I noticed several places where the prophet or apostle, who is supposed to be writing as the Holy Spirit dictated, actually doubts that what he is writing is true.

At my first thumbing through the New Testament section of *The Message* and finding some parts rather disturbing, I flipped to the Old Testament, and without even turning one page, my eyes fell on Jeremiah 2, which corresponded to verses 23–24, in the KJV:

> How canst thou say, I am not polluted, I have not gone after Baalim? see thy way in the valley, know what thou hast done: thou art a swift

dromedary traversing her ways; A wild ass used to the wilderness, thou snuffeth up the wind at her pleasure; in her occasion who can turn her away? all they that seek her will not weary themselves; in her month they shall find her.

Now read these same verses from *The Message*:

How dare you tell me, "I'm not stained by sin. I've never chased after the Baal sex gods!" Well, look at the tracks you've left behind in the valley. How do you account for what is written in the desert dust—tracks of a camel in heat, running this way and that, tracks of a wild donkey in rut, sniffing the wind for the slightest scent of sex. Who could possibly corral her! On the hunt for sex, sex, and more sex—insatiable, indiscriminate, promiscuous.

The gutter language in parts of *The Message* I would think would be offensive to many adults, much less teenagers. Maybe this is the way some of the unchurched, or even the churched, talk today, but I do not think this is the way that Christians should communicate.

Let your speech be alway with grace. . . .

—Colossians 4:6

Let no corrupt communication proceed out of your mouth. . . .

—Ephesians 4:29

There is a way, as indicated in the King James Version, that we can express God's displeasure with an immoral personal relationship between a man and a woman without using contemporary three-letter and four-letter words.

As with *The Message*, I personally think that all non-literal, paraphrased modern versions should be labeled and promoted as commentaries, not Bibles. However, I would be less than honest if I did not report that parts of *The Message* were better than some of the other paraphrased versions. Of course, some were worse. The same thing would be true of *The Purpose Driven Life* and the entire ministry of Dr. Rick Warren who uses and recommends *The Message*. Anything that sells, and especially new Christian programs and movements, have to be based on tenets that appear biblically productive. A totally bad product or program will not be accepted or bought by anyone.

Let us suppose that a salesman came to your door with a huge box of freshly baked cookies. The cookies are beautiful and smell delicious. As you appear interested, the salesman offers to sell you enough for the whole church for only $1,000. (This is approximately what the PDL programs cost each church).

You say, "But what are the dark spots in the cookies?"

The salesman responds, "Oh, the cookies are made out of the finest flour, sugars, and spices available. However, 20 percent of the cookies' volume is cow manure."

You say, "But how will the church members eat those cookies with the manure in them?"

The salesman answers, "No problem. Just tell them to spit out the dark spots of the cow manure and eat the rest of the cookie."

The reader will probably conclude that this is a terrible example, which it is. But what about the seventy thousand pastors who have disseminated copies of *The Purpose Driven Life* to their memberships that encourage replacing the Authorized Version Bibles with *The Message*? Have they no responsibility?

As I stated in chapter two, church-based spiritual movements, some good and some not so good, sweep through Christendom from time to time. Some pass in due course without any lasting effect and some, like the charismatic movement, leave behind continuing evidence, but the majority of the church establishments move on without change. The purpose driven church movement, however, is the most inclusive paradigm shift in Christendom since the Protestant Reformation.

Will the new church growth movement that generally gets its energy from the purpose driven church and Mr. Murdoch's billions really make Jesus Christ more acceptable to the world's unchurched? Or will the doctrineless church majority and the unchurched who are seeking a bloodless-redemption religion join together to bring in the false church of Mr. Antichrist? Is it possible that we are on the brink of the great falling away that is referenced in 2 Thessalonians 2? These are questions that may be answered in coming months or years.

Where Have All the Doctrines Gone?

The trio of Peter, Paul, and Mary back in the '60s popularized an anti-Vietnam War song with the lyrics:

> *Where have all the young men gone?*
> *Gone for soldiers every one.*
> *Where have all the soldiers gone?*
> *Gone to graveyards every one.*
> *When will they ever learn?*

When this song was popular, I was teaching Sunday school and training union at the First Baptist Church of Nicoma Park, Oklahoma. The teaching of the fundamentals of the Christian faith within the eight basic Bible doctrines was an essential of both Sunday school and pulpit presentation, not only among Southern Baptists, but most other flavors of Baptists, and other denominations as well. Also at that time, doctrine was still an essential of most seminary curriculums.

Why is doctrine important? If our Christian faith is built upon sound and unchanging doctrinal pillars as set forth by God in His Word, then we will not be "carried about with every wind of doctrine" (Eph. 4:14). As instructed in 2 Timothy 3:10, if a Christian is well grounded in sound doctrine, then he or she will not be deceived by false teachers and every new cult that comes along. It has been reported that half of the Jehovah's Witness cult are former Southern Baptists, and now almost 100 percent of Southern Baptist churches, and probably the majority of churches of other denominations, have embraced some form of the purpose driven church movement.

To explain the eight doctrinal pillars of the Christian faith would take an entire book; however, we list them with a brief comment, because most church members today do not even know what they are:

1. **Theism:** The reality of God and His revelation in Three Persons.
2. **Bibliology:** The divine revelation of God to mankind in the sixty-six books of the Bible, written by men led and inspired by the Holy Spirit, authoritative and infallible.
3. **Theology:** God as Creator by Jesus Christ; the laws of God that govern this world and the universe.
4. **Angelology:** The creation and mission of angels; classification, missions, and future of those who fell, and those who remained faithful to God.
5. **Anthropology:** The creation of man, his fall, and inherent carnality; the reality of Heaven for redeemed man; the reality of Hell for the lost.
6. **Soteriology:** Jesus Christ; His preincarnate appearances; His incarnation as both God and man in the form of man; His death in sinful man's place; salvation by faith in Jesus Christ, a gift of God's grace; the new birth and ministry of the Holy Spirit; sanctification—immediate and progressive; rewards and the Judgment Seat of Christ.
7. **Ecclesiology:** Church definition; founding of the church; government of the church; church ordinances; mission of the church, now and in the future.
8. **Eschatology:** The Second Coming of Jesus Christ; purpose of His

return; the Rapture or Translation of the church; resurrections; judgments; the coming Kingdom age; the New Heaven and the New Earth.

Mr. Rick Warren on page 34 of his book *The Purpose Driven Life* states:

> One day you will stand before God, and he will do an audit of your life, a final exam, before you enter eternity. The Bible says, "Remember, each of us will stand personally before the judgment seat of God. . . . Yes, each of us will have to give a personal account to God." Fortunately, God wants us to pass this test, so he has given us the questions in advance. From the Bible we can surmise that God will ask us two crucial questions. First, "What did you do with my Son, Jesus Christ." God won't ask about your religious background or doctrinal views. The only thing that will matter is, did you accept what Jesus did for you and did you learn to love and trust him?

Mr. Warren quotes Romans 14:10 from one of the new versions. The NIV, NASV, and the HCSB, and almost all the other new versions, with the exception of the NKJV, say "the judgment seat of God." We read in John 5:22 that the Father has committed all judgment to the Son. Paul stated in Romans 14:10, and repeats in 2 Corinthians 5:10, that we, meaning all Christians, must appear before the Judgment Seat of Christ to be judged, not for salvation, but for rewards. The Textus Receptus states plainly, the Judgment Seat of *Christos,* interpreted correctly in the KJV as Christ. The word is *Christos,* not *Theos.* We are not going to be asked about our relationship with Jesus Christ, because if we were not saved, we would not be before the Judgment Seat of Christ in the first place. Perhaps Mr. Warren thinks he is to appear for judgment before the Great White Throne Judgment. If he thinks that, then he is in a lot of trouble. He continues to indicate that salvation also depends upon learning to love and trust Jesus experientially. This is a progressive salvation teaching and is contrary to sound doctrine, but Mr. Warren indicates that doctrine is not important. And tens of thousands of pastors are insisting that their memberships read Mr. Warren's books and espouse this kind of fuzzy, confusing heresy.

In the Old Testament we find the word "doctrine" six times in the KJV as translated from the Masoretic Text. Two different Hebrew words were understood to be doctrine in the context. In the NIV, NASV, and the HCSB, these words are translated to be: "teaching," seven times; "beliefs," once; "instruction," four times; "message," twice; "taught," once; "discipline," once; "instructed," once; and "instruct," once. Now we would think that in just one of the eighteen places the new versions would take into consideration that for over four hundred years millions of Christian scholars and laymen had understood these words to mean doctrine. But no, the word "doctrine" must go.

But you say, what difference does it make if the Scripture says doctrine, teaching, instruction, or message? Let's continue and go to the New Testament.

In the New Testament, the word "doctrine" occurs forty-four times in the singular in the KJV. The Greek word for "doctor" in the Received Text is *didaskalos*. The Greek word for "doctrine" is *didaskalia*. There is no excuse for translating *didaskalia* as teaching, beliefs, message, or instruction. Your doctor may instruct you to take prescribed medicine, or he may try to teach you how to take care of your health. But teaching or instructing are not the doctor, any more than teaching or instruction is doctrine. Discipleship, or teaching and instruction, come from doctrine.

We read in the four Gospels that the masses were amazed at the doctrine of Jesus Christ, and "doctrine" is found in the singular twelve times in the Gospels. Now we might think that in at least one place the NIV, NASV, or the HCSB would translate from the Westcott and Hort text the word "doctrine." Think again—it isn't there. In all twelve places, all three versions substitute "teaching" for doctrine. Coincidence? No!

In the book of Acts "doctrine" is mentioned four times. Again, the NIV, NASV, and the HCSB say "teaching"—not "doctrine." I understand that the HCSB is not referenced in *The Purpose Driven Life,* probably because it was not published when Dr. Warren was writing it, if indeed Dr. Warren really did write it. Some noted ministers, I know for fact, pay others to write their books. I am not saying this is the case with Dr. Warren, but I know it does occur. I use the HCSB as an example in this chapter to illustrate a trend, as the HCSB is one of the very latest new versions.

In the general epistles, "doctrine" is mentioned nine times in the KJV. In the other versions referenced, the Greek is translated "teaching," "instruction," or "message." Finally, the NASV in Ephesians 4:14 translated the Greek to mean "doctrine." In the pastoral epistles, the KJV references "doctrine" sixteen times, and finally the new Westcott and Hort versions do relent somewhat, possibly to avoid conservative criticism of the heavily doctrinal epistles. In the pastoral epistles, of the sixteen times "doctrine" is mentioned, the NIV translates the word "doctrine" seven times, and "teaching" nine times; the NASV, "doctrine" eight times, "teaching" eight times; the HCSB, "doctrine" only three times, "teaching" thirteen times. The NIV claims dynamic equivalency. The HCSB claims optimal equivalency—some option. In the three scriptures in Revelation where the word "doctrine" appears, "teaching" has taken its place in all three versions, as in all Westcott and Hort newer versions. Our associate ministers provide further insight as to why doctrines are being depleted from the newer versions of the Bible:

Doctrine, Proof-texting, and Modern Versions

If you have ever tried to compare a racy, modern version of the Bible with the Authorized Version to see how the modern version renders a certain verse, you have encountered some major difficulties. Verse divisions are often omitted and phrases are often scrambled. Sometimes the modern paraphrase is so far removed from the AV that you've even asked yourself, "Is this the right chapter?" Might this have anything to do with the current war against Bible doctrine?

Modernists don't like to talk about "doctrine." Neither do they like proof-texting, the accepted method for establishing any doctrine. A proof-text is a Bible verse, or portion of Scripture, that provides the biblical basis for a doctrine. Because doctrine allegedly divides, those who use proof-texting to establish a doctrine are ridiculed. The modernists' solution to proof-texting is to publish a version that makes proof-texting impossible.

The Message is a prime example of how a particular Bible version is being used to weaken churches and to allow false and dangerous doctrines to be accepted by the masses of undiscerning church members.

—Dr. Larry Spargimino

Comparison of KJV and Other Versions

When comparing a certain word that appears in the KJV with the same word in other versions, it is necessary to check the phrases in each to make sure you are dealing with the same word. For instance, in most cases the NIV, NASV, and the HCSB use the word "teaching" instead of the word "doctrine" used in the KJV. The other versions, especially the NIV and HCSB, are so convoluted that it is difficult to know if you are comparing the same word. The word "doctrine" appears fifty times in the KJV, but only thirteen times in the NASV; seven times in the NIV; and six times in the HCSB in comparing the same verses.

It appears that doctrine is less and less important as the newer versions appear. It is obvious that most of these word changes were made only to add to the number of word changes for copyright purposes. While all of the anti-KJV versions are guilty, the HCSB translates the same Greek New Testament word as "doctrine" in 2 Timothy 4:3 and "teaching" in Titus 1:9, revealing that they do realize that there is a difference, but deliberately create confusion.

In the PDC churches there is a move to remove denominational titles, doctrines, and even the name "church." Doctrinal substance appears less and less in Sunday school materials or presented from the pulpit. Most churches now frown upon anything that is fundamental doctrinally. We are even told that doctrine is divisive, bad, or evil. If the word "doctrine" is taken from the Bible, then the doctrines of God can be completely eliminated.

—Dr. Bob Glaze

For the time will come when they will not endure sound doctrine; but after their own lusts shall they heap to themselves teachers, having itching ears; And they shall turn away their ears from the truth, and shall be turned unto fables.

—2 Timothy 4:3–4

Where have all the doctrines gone?
Gone from our Bibles, every one.
Where have all the Christians gone?
Gone in the Rapture, every one.
When will they ever learn?
When will they ever learn?

Letters from listeners

Dear Dr. Hutchings:

Your recent letter was partly a surprise in that you told us that the church to which you were accustomed, and had been a long-term member, no longer welcomed your presence. It is shocking!

Our local church took up the "40 days of purpose" and we are having some tense times. There is a small cadre (of three people) in the staff who want to bring our church "up to date" *a la* Willow Creek, which is an off-shoot of Saddleback, etc.

If your staff prays for individual churches, please add us to your prayer list.

I am retired, however, I still have some connections via my engineering associations and I wondered which big corporations and which network is so supportive of Rick Warren. I'd like to give somebody a shock from the other direction!!

All of the strange happenings remind me of a remark I heard, "We are not promised a smooth ride as Christians, just a safe landing."

Our Lord's return for the church is near.

—From J.S. / Madison Heights., Michigan

Dear Dr. Hutchings:

We are glad to send you our check for $15.00 to help you with your fight against the purpose driven church movement. I wish I could send more—but I'm 91 now with very little income, and this is the best we can do to help financially.

I am one of the "dislocated ones" as a result of my outspoken opposition to Rick Warren's book that our ---------- Church here in Portland adopted for an all-church project last year. I had been teaching an adult Bible Class for the past twelve years, acceptably so, as far as I could tell, but when I refused to cooperate with the church program, a few in the class created enough fuss that I was asked to leave—so I did. Warren's program is an insidious product of Satan, Himself. Obviously, the closer we get to the end, the harder he will be fighting!

We pray that our Lord will encourage and strengthen you—and others—to continue your work.

—E.D.P. / Portland, Oregon

Dr. Hutchings wanted some input as to what we are experiencing in our local churches with the purpose driven life/church. Let me begin by saying that my husband and I read a book entitled, *And The Shofar Blew* by Francine Rivers about this very thing happening in the churches. We began to take note of some of the church being the most obvious. However, in the past three years since we have joined this new church these things have gone on:

1. Teaching the virgin birth is a theory and that Jesus could have been just divinely chosen.

2. Taking the whole Sunday school hour to do a class on "Different Religions of the World." This was NOT from the viewpoint of someone who had become a Christian, these were Muslims, Buddhists, and Jewish persons. (My husband and I opted NOT to attend or allow our children to attend. We had Sunday school for the three others who did not choose to go and my children came to the adult class).

3. My pastor is teaching *The Purpose Driven Life,* along with his wife. Can you advise me on what is happening?

Thank you for taking the time to read and answer my questions. God bless you for your dedication to the Truth.

—e-mail from B.N.

Dear Brother Hutchings:

Just like you, we have been forced to leave our church because of Rick Warren and his P.D.C. program. We are now looking for another church, and I'm sure that I don't have to tell you how we feel.

We are an older couple—we have been married fifty years, been around long enough to appreciate a ministry such as yours. We have several of your books and have ordered many books and tapes from SWRC. We have received the *Prophetic Observer* for years. We recently ordered *Deceived on Purpose* by Warren Smith and *Who's*

Driving the Purpose Driven Church? by James Sundquist. Wonderful books, helped us in our decision to leave our church.

Just wanted to say, "Thank You" for your ministry. We have always admired you. Keep up the good work. God bless you and your ministry.

—W. & J.C.

Dear Sirs:

I was reading your purpose driven church article in your February newsletter! We have been without a church for five years ever since this Rick Warren PDC started. I agree that it is based on religious deception. The other thing I notice that he does is take all the new so-called versions of the Bible and quote from the one or ones when put together makes the scriptures say what he wants them to say. You keep your promise to the Lord. Satan sees the time is short and wants to take as many as possible with him. Let's keep the faith and the word sound.

—e-mail from L.M.T. & J.T. / Colorado

Hello, my name is P.J. and I attend ---------- Covenant Church in Hutchinson, MN. Our church is picking up on the "purpose driven church" fad and we are already seeing the cracks. Three churches in our little town of 11k have split because of this book.

Our pastor says, "Yes, people have expressed concern that this book contains false teaching but so far no one has proven it to me."

This man is supposed to have all this teaching, and me with my two years of Bible school at a conservative Lutheran school, plus years of teaching at my dad's knee (sometimes as a not very willing student) and I can see what's wrong with it.

My question is, how do I as well as the handful of other people that know this book is off the mark confront this . . . "heresy"? My husband just bought two of the books listed on your site, *Who's Driving* and *Deceived on Purpose*. I am presently going through Rick Warren's book writing notes in the margins as they occur to me . . . which is quite often.

I see you have lots of material I could order, but wonder which would be the most effective and how we should present it.

—e-mail from P.J. / Hutchinson, Minnesota

Chapter 6

Trying the Spirits

of the Purpose Driven Church Religion

Beloved, believe not every spirit, but try the spirits whether they are of God. . . . Hereby know ye the Spirit of God: Every spirit that confesseth that Jesus Christ is come in the flesh is of God: And every spirit that confesseth not that Jesus Christ is come in the flesh is not of God. . . .

—1 John 4:1–3

Now the Spirit speaketh expressly, that in the latter times some shall depart from the faith, giving heed to seducing spirits, and doctrines of devils; Speaking lies in hypocrisy; having their conscience seared with a hot iron.

—1 Timothy 4:1–2

Every Christian, and particularly every pastor and minister, has a responsibility to test the spirits of every religious fad or change that attempts to invade the church. This is not an option; it is a commandment. The greatest danger to the church, as we read in the New Testament, is not from outside oppression, aggression, or martyrdom; it is from those who would rise up from inside the church.

Take heed therefore unto yourselves, and to all the flock, over the which the Holy Ghost hath made you overseers, to feed the church of God, which he hath purchased with his own blood. For I know this, that after my departing shall grievous wolves enter in among you, not sparing the flock. Also of your own selves shall men arise, speaking perverse things, to draw away disciples after them.

—Acts 20:28–30

For there must be also heresies among you, that they which are approved may be made manifest among you.

—1 Corinthians 11:19

But though we, or an angel from heaven, preach any other gospel unto you than that which we have preached unto you, let him be accursed.

—Galatians 1:8

O foolish Galatians, who hath bewitched you, that ye should not obey the truth, before whose eyes Jesus Christ hath been evidently set forth, crucified among you?

—Galatians 3:1

But there were false prophets also among the people, even as there shall be false teachers among you, who privily shall bring in damnable heresies, even denying the Lord that bought them, and bring upon themselves swift destruction. And many shall follow their pernicious ways; by reason of whom the way of truth shall be evil spoken of. And through covetousness shall they with feigned words make merchandise of you: whose judgment now of a long time lingereth not, and their damnation slumbereth not.

—2 Peter 2:1–3

Knowing this first, that there shall come in the last days scoffers, walking after their own lusts, And saying, Where is the promise of his coming? for since the fathers fell asleep, all things continue as they were from the beginning of the creation.

—2 Peter 3:3–4

Whosoever transgresseth, and abideth not in the doctrine of Christ, hath not God. He that abideth in the doctrine of Christ, he hath both the Father and the Son. If there come any unto you, and bring not this doctrine, receive him not into your house, neither bid him God speed:

—2 John 9–10

For there are certain men crept in unawares, who were before of old ordained to this condemnation, ungodly men, turning the grace of our God into lasciviousness, and denying the only Lord God, and our Lord Jesus Christ.

—Jude 4

Every church or Christian organization does, or should, have a public statement of faith so that anyone who is interested can know what that entity believes and teaches. However, such statements of faith are often for public notice and not necessarily the practiced convictions of the organization and the founder or leader. Also, such affirmations of reported beliefs may change without notice. In any event, as noted, it is the individual's responsibility, if a Christian, to know wherein the church or organization they belong to or contribute support stands on basic Bible doctrines relating to salvation and ministering in the name of their Saviour and Lord, Jesus Christ.

When we checked Saddleback's web site in May 2005 we found a brief roster of ten items of belief to which Dr. Warren evidently ascribes. These ten items are listed in order with my brief comment. I will take an additional look at the expanded explanation on the Saddleback web site following, and I can accept that Dr. Warren probably wrote these ten items himself; although, I have serious doubts about the expanded list.

What Dr. Warren Believes

To test the spirits of the PDC church growth phenomenon, I obtained a copy of the Saddleback Church's statement of faith, except it is called "What We Believe." By "we," I suppose this is what Dr. Warren believes, as he is aided by staff members whom he hired and can fire at will. The PDC "Believe" statement reads:

1. **God is bigger and greater and closer than we can imagine.** I never thought of God getting bigger and better, like a Burger King Whopper. I always think of God as Alpha and Omega, and everything in between.

2. **Jesus is God showing Himself to us.** This is an interesting and simple explanation of just who Jesus is; however, to me, Dr. Warren has an annoying habit of leaving "Christ" off after the name of Jesus. Jesus, as we read in *Young's Concordance,* was His common name; and there have been many men with this name. But Jesus Christ is the only "God-anointed Saviour" who was sacrificed in our place for our sins.

3. **Through the Holy Spirit, God lives in and through us now.** While the expanded explanation in another section explains the Trinity, the statement that the Holy Spirit lives within a person "the moment they decide to follow Him" is not only ambiguous, it is not biblical. The unbeliever, or the unsaved, is born again of the Holy Spirit when he or she puts their faith in Jesus Christ who died for their sins on the cross. It seems to me that Dr. Warren here places doubt on the new birth.

4. **The Bible is God's perfect workbook for living.** This weak affirmation of the Bible as God's inspired and infallible Word is

amended and strengthened in the expanded explanation. However, in his book *The Purpose Driven Life*, Dr. Warren quotes from fourteen different and mostly newer versions of the Bible, based on the Westcott and Hort New Testament of 1881, a total of 628 scriptures. Included in this list are paraphrased versions like *The Message* where the author himself, Dr. Peterson, said it should not be considered God's Word. It has been noted by others that Dr. Warren uses the many translations in order to find a scripture that says what he wants it to say. In other words, God is agreeing with him rather than he is agreeing with God. I seem to remember another instance in the Bible where this occurred. If Dr. Warren thinks the Bible is the perfect guide, then he must think his books are even more perfect, because he states that church members study their Bibles too much and that they should study his book. Listeners living near Saddleback have reported to us they never see members taking a Bible to church, and one pastor visiting the church reported he saw only three Bible in the entire congregation.

5. **Nothing is creation "just happened." God made it all.** In six days? In six thousand years? In six million years? In six billion years? The expanded explanation does not say, either.

6. **Grace is the only way to have a relationship with God.** Grace is unmerited or unearned favor. All are sinners and undeserving of God's forgiveness. We are all cut off from God, but a sinner can receive forgiveness by accepting Jesus Christ by faith who paid the penalty for sin by His own blood on the cross. Without Jesus Christ, a sinner has no relationship with God. This ambiguous explanation about the way of salvation is one of the most serious errors of the Church Growth movement.

7. **Faith is the only way to grow in our relationship with God.** We read in Ephesians 2:8–9: "For by grace are ye saved through faith; and that not of yourselves: it is the gift of God: Not of works, lest

any man should boast." Grace is mentioned thirty-eight times in the Old Testament, usually in reference to a favor granted by a king or landlord. Grace is mentioned four times in the Gospels, but ninety times in the Pauline epistles, where it references that we gentiles who had no covenant, promise, sabbath days, feast days, tabernacle, or temple, by God's undeserved favor and love we can be saved by faith in what His Son did for us in dying in our place. But in Dr. Warren's statements of faith and subsequent qualifications, he always attaches modifying conjunctions or adverbs, *and . . . if . . . or . . .* Usually, these qualifications or additions have something to do with the PDC programs, so the PDC constituent has to do what God says, and then do what Dr. Warren says. And even so, the one thing that is absent from the pronouncements and affirmations in the Saddleback and Willow Creek websites, literature, and books, is concern for those, including the elderly, who are either leaving or being kicked out of their churches due to PDC super-marketing programs. "Though I speak with the tongues of men and of angels, and have not charity, I am become as sounding brass, or a tinkling cymbal. And though I have the gift of prophecy, and understand all mysteries, and all knowledge; and though I have all faith, so that I could remove mountains, and have not charity, I am nothing" (1 Cor. 13:1–2).

8. **God has allowed evil to provide us with a choice. God can bring good even out of evil events and God promises victory over evil to those who choose Him.** This confusing explanation of evil by Dr. Warren gives us a choice to be evil or good, but we do not have a choice. Paul explains in Romans 3 that all men and women are born sinners and there is none good, not even one. Our only choice is to either accept Jesus Christ who died for our sins and put on His righteousness, or continue in sin and be forever separated from God in Hell. To choose Jesus Christ, not because we had to, but because we freely decided to do so, is the

only glory that God does not already have.

9. **Heaven and Hell are real places. Death is a beginning, not an end.** We find no fault with this statement, except to point out that if both Heaven and Hell are real places, then the first letter in both words should be capitalized. We would also point out that the majority of new Bible versions that Dr. Warren references in *The Purpose Driven Life* omit Hell all thirty-one times it is found in the Authorized Version in the Old Testament, and 50 percent of the times in the New Testament.

10. **Jesus is coming again.** In the purpose driven church explanation, nothing is presented about the signs of the times in which Jesus will return; nothing about the Rapture or translation of the church; nothing is said about the millennial reign or the Kingdom age. Dr. Warren evidently accepts the replacement theology, preterist, A-millennial position. The only reason for Jesus coming again according to PDC eschatology is to bring an end to the world, which is a doctrinal position that most evangelical, fundamental churches would reject if they would really inform themselves about PDC theology.

In the roster of "beliefs" of Dr. Warren, there is nothing about the cross; nothing about the blood; and nothing about the new birth. This would indicate that the purpose driven church religion is primarily a works-based religion rather than a faith-based way of salvation.

Saddleback's Expanded Roster of Beliefs

As already noted in this chapter, I can believe that Dr. Warren wrote the brief ten item roster of Saddleback's and his beliefs, but it is most difficult for me to believe that he wrote the twelve items expanded explanations. They are too well written. I would expect that Richard Abanes or one of the Saddleback staff wrote it. In any event, we submit these added comments:

1. **What is the Bible?** In the expanded explanation we read: "Every word of scripture is chosen by God himself . . . the final authority in every issue it communicates. It is complete truth." Does this mean the original documents? Does it mean in every version Dr. Warren uses, like *The Message*? Eusebius compiled for Constantine the manuscripts that Origen edited. Origen believed in universal salvation, that even the devil would be saved. Most newer versions of the Bible are based on these texts.

2. **Who is God?** Other than our previous comment on this item, we have little to offer further. In this expanded explanation, God is presented as Creator and Trinity. However, the threefold nature of God (omniscient, omnipotent, omnipresent) is not mentioned, but this could have been an oversight. Twenty-seven scriptures are listed to support the purpose driven church's explanation of God, and probably ten or more referenced Him as Creator. Scriptures indicating that God created the world, the universe, and all things therein in six days are avoided.

3. **Who is Jesus?** In answer to this question we read from the expanded explanation by Saddleback (Dr. Warren): "Jesus Christ is God's Son and *an* equal of the Father" (emphasis on *an* added). In the first place, it would have been better had a definite article like *the* preceded "equal." The way this statement reads could be interpreted to mean there are many "equals" with the Father. Also, Jesus is God's only begotten (conceived) Son, not just God's Son. Adam is a son by direct creation (Luke 3:38). The angels are sons of God by direct creation (Job 2:1). Christians are sons of God by a spiritual new birth (John 3:5–7; Rom. 8:11–17; 1 John 3:1–2). Dr. Warren (or someone) also did not remember that Jesus Christ was born of a virgin.

4. **Who is the Holy Spirit?** We read the first sentence in the explanation: "The Holy Spirit is a full and equal part of the Trinity." RIGHT —Dr. Warren and staff at Saddleback get an "A". Next

we read, "He works in the world to make all people understand their need for Jesus Christ." Only part right, they get a "C". The Holy Spirit convicts the conscience of men and women of sin. It is the church's business to tell them how to get forgiveness of that sin through faith in Jesus Christ who died in their place.

And next we read, "The Holy Spirit lives inside every follower of Jesus from the moment they decide to follow Him." WRONG—"F" "F" "F." A spiritual new birth occurs when, by "faith," a sinner receives Jesus Christ as Saviour (Eph. 1:12–15). When Jesus told Nicodemus that he must be born again of the Spirit, the Lord continued and told him how to get that new birth in John 3:16. It was by faith, not by works. It is true that Christians are encouraged to a closer walk with the Lord Jesus Christ to be filled with the Spirit, but how can a Christian be filled with the Spirit if they have not already been born of the Spirit. Here, I think Dr. Warren (or whoever at Saddleback) is denying the spiritual new birth.

Dr. Warren stretches his statement of doctrinal beliefs, or lack thereof, so that it will be acceptable to as many different denominations as possible so they will, if possible, become purpose driven churches, buy his books, and buy his programs for forty days at various levels. And, it is a common law of physics that the farther you stretch a rubber band, the weaker it gets in the middle.

5. **What is Man?** Man is explained as God's highest order of creation, but it seems that man has a bad attitude, and "this attitude also keeps us from being the kind of person God created us to be." While this explanation might reach a five-year-old, I question if it would bring an adult under the conviction of his sinful, lost condition and need for repentance.

Items six through ten are Saddleback's, and I presume also Dr. Warren's beliefs and understandings about salvation, security of the believer and Heaven. As an adult, it is difficult for me to relate to something that seems to be written at the first or second grade level. "When I was a child, I spake as a child, I understood as a child, I thought as a child: but when I became a man . . ." (1 Cor. 13:11). In these sections, the rule that Dr. Warren will not stress doctrine or say something that might offend seems to have been followed. I was not surprised that little was noted about either sin or Hell in specifics. Had I considered these items individually, I probably would be more critical than they might deserve.

6. **What is the Second Coming of Jesus?** Comment: The brief explanation of the purpose driven church's understanding of eschatology is: "God in His own time and in His own way, will bring the world to its appropriate end. According to His promise, Jesus Christ will return personally and visibly in glory to the earth; the dead will be raised; and Christ will judge all men in righteousness." Today we live in a world where it is more difficult to raise children and protect them from pornography, crime, and fear than ever before. We live in a time where the world's brain trust in regards to our future existence predict that there is a 70 percent chance that there will be nuclear war in the next ten years. Knowledge has increased and men are running to and fro, violence and fear grips the hearts of men as Jesus and the prophets foretold.

Israel is a nation again after two thousand years, and Jerusalem is a burdensome stone for all nations as is prophesied (Zech. 12). Dr. Warren follows the excuse that Jesus said that no man could know the day or the hour of His return, but He admonished that we could know when His coming was near, even at the doors. Paul said "that day" should not overtake Christians as a thief in the night, and Peter advised that we could know the coming of the Lord was near by the fulfillment of prophetic signs: "Knowing this first [importance], that there shall come in the last days scoffers, walking [proclaiming] after their lusts [greeds], and saying, Where is the promise [signs] of his coming? . . ." (2 Pet. 3:3–4).

Dr. Warren ignores the scriptures that admonish Christians to watch and be ready for the Lord's return (1 Thess. 5:23; 2 Pet. 3; Rev. 3:3). He also either appears ignorant, or confused, about the chronology of resurrection:

> And I saw the [lost] dead, small and great, stand before God, and the books were opened; and another book was opened: which is the book of life: and the [lost] dead were judged out of those things which were written in the books, according to their works, And the sea gave up the [lost] dead which were in it; and death and hell delivered up the [lost] dead which were in them: and they [lost dead] were judged every man according to their works. And death and hell were cast into the lake of fire. This is the second death. And whosoever was not found written in the book of life was cast into the lake of fire.
>
> —Revelation 20:12–15

As mentioned before, nowhere does Dr. Warren reference the Christians standing before Jesus Christ to receive a reward for their service; or Jesus Christ returning to destroy the Antichrist and his armies; or to reign over the nations for a thousand years, and leaders of the nations coming to worship Him; or Jesus bringing peace to the world for a thousand years. Evidently, Dr. Warren has his own agenda to end war, famine, crime, and bring peace on earth. Quoting Dr. Warren from his April 17, 2005, Anaheim Declaration:

> Our goal will be to enlist one billion foot soldiers for the Kingdom of God, who will permanently change the face of international missions to take on these five "global giants for which the church can

become the ultimate distribution and change agent to overcome Spiritual Emptiness, Self-serving Leadership, Poverty, Disease and Ignorance.

If Dr. Warren actually believes that he and his purpose driven church are going to eliminate war, hunger, disease, crime, and ignorance, then he needs to write his own bible. I don't read about anything like this at all happening in these last days. I read that there will be wars and rumors of wars until Christ returns; there will be famines and disease epidemics of pandemic proportions; evil men and seducers will wax worse and worse; men will be lovers of their own selves, and the unsaved world will cry peace but there will be no peace.

I certainly admire Dr. Warren's vision and courage, but I know of others who have dreamed the same dream. However, they haven't sold thirty million books; in fact, I doubt if they sold any books at all. Their sphere of activity was limited to a rather restricted department in a local hospital.

I received a letter dated June 2005 from S.E.D. of Dallas:

Dr. Hutchings:

I enjoy reading your *Prophetic Observer* newsletter whenever it comes out and couldn't agree with you more about the effects of Rick Warren and his purpose driven hoo-ha. A couple of weeks ago Mr. Warren came to Dallas and the *Morning News* conducted an interview with him. In talking to friends and family they suggested that I send you a copy of the article. If it wasn't so sad that people fall hook, line, and sinker for this guy, it would be laughable.

The secular influence on the Church is not good, and you articulate the reasons so eloquently in your *Prophetic Observer* newsletter. My thanks to you and your organization for the work you are doing. Always remember that you are not alone in your fight.

Sincerely.

The article enclosed was from the May 16, 2005, edition of the *Dallas Morning News*. Quoting Dr. Warren from the article:

> I was recently in Africa, working in orphanages and meeting with presidents. And I recently spoke at Harvard. I got there expecting a debate, and instead I found, "Tell me more...." I got a letter from Hindus, from Muslims . . . it's cross cultural. . . . My goal is the second Reformation of the church. . . . The first Reformation was about creeds. This one is about deeds [works]. I've been training pastors—400,000 from around the world.

Eve added five little words to God's commandment in regards to eating the fruit of the tree of knowledge of good and evil: ". . . neither shall ye touch it." When we lie we become susceptible to the devil's lie: "Ye shall be as gods, knowing good and evil." In other words, the devil makes us think we do not need God to tell us how to run our lives. The devil has never changed his lie because he hasn't had to—it works over and over.

It is true what Dr. Warren says on pages 9–10 concerning forty days: it did rain forty days after Noah entered the ark; Moses did spend forty days on Mount Sinai; twelve spies did spend forty days in the Promised Land. It is not true that the forty days transformed their lives. Therefore, in my opinion, the entire book is based on an untruth. I would say lie, but I do not want to offend Dr. Warren.

While all judgment has been committed to Jesus Christ by the Father (John 5:22), as responsible Christians we are to "try the spirits" whether they are of God, or . . .

We understand that the purpose driven church is the greatest paradigm shift in the church since Martin Luther's Ninety-Five Theses five hundred years ago. We understand that Dr. Warren has done great things and has planned even greater things, but we also read in Isaiah

14:13 that a spirit being once said, "I will exalt my throne above the stars of God."

More Letters

Following are just a few more of the hundreds of letters we have received from Christians who are leaving purpose driven churches. I have not attempted to choose a certain type of letter, but picked them out one after another. I cannot, of course, include the multitude of letters and e-mails received on this subject, but this cross section should give the reader, and pastors, evidence that all is not light and glory in PDC congregations and there is a darker side to this cultic movement.

Dear Brother Hutchings:

I am one of many concerned Christians in regarding our churches. We stopped going to our Cornerstone Church because the music was so loud. The minister said to put cotton in my ears. We sat at the back thinking that would help. To be told to just stick it in your ears just was not the thing to say.

You hit the nail on the head about the music. Some think they have to put the people into a frenzy for the SPIRIT TO FALL!

May God bless your ministry. Thank you for telling the truth.

In Christ,

V.V. / Quinlan, Texas

Dear Pastor Hutchings & Staff:

We so enjoy the programs and the people on your broadcast who are recognizing the movement on the purpose driven church. So thankful that Christians are coming out of it. It is pure deception.

So thankful that our God opens our eyes to the apostate churches. Surely these are the last days. We thank God for your programs to stand up for the true Word of God and the hymns. We too have left churches in the past due mainly to the music.

I wonder why more pastors do not recognize this as pagan? I did read recently the *Prophetic Observer* on "Trying the Spirits." Pastor Hutchings—I've listened to your program a long time—and I appreciate all of you taking a stand against the enemy. I wish more people knew the King James Bible and how they too can be blessed by the "True Word" of God.

This year we plan to attend your meetings in Oklahoma City. Looking forward to them. When we attend the meetings we can bring home a lot of books and tapes and be a witness to others—to show them the way also. I wish everyone could see this New Age doctrine and how evil it has become. The deception that lies within its roots.

I must close—but wanted you to know my husband and I remain Watchmen on the Wall.

God bless you all.

> Love
>
> P.M. / Devine, Texas

Greetings:

I would like to order four of your books, *The Paganization of Music,* by Dr. Jack Wheaton #2—I have #1 for this reason.

Our church has over one thousand members. About eight years ago our pastor went to L.A. to look into the purpose driven church program. When he came back it wasn't long before we dropped the evening service, removed the organ, and removed the hymn books.

Our platform looks more like a night club than a church. We finally let our pastor go because he wanted to be more like a dictator than a pastor.

We just came back from a prophetic conference with Dr. Jimmy DeYoung. I asked him about Rick Warren. His answer was don't ask. I like what you stand for—keep it up.

Thanks and keep looking up,

F.H. / Mount Vernon, Washington

Dear Pastor Hutchings:

Thank you so much for your enduring work for the Lord. I especially appreciate your newsletter and its information. The information you gave made me able to see the beginnings of the insidious purpose driven church in my local church. I live in South Orange County not far from the Saddleback Church where this started. Now our Elders' Board has pushed out our fine Bible-teaching pastor and is embracing this. The congregation is splitting and it's very chaotic. Please pray for us. It's a non-denominational evangelical church so there is no outside control on these people.

May God's will be done!

Sincerely,

G.P. / California

Dear Brother Hutchings:

I recently had occasion to attend several classes covering the entire book sponsored by the purpose driven church. The text did violence to the Scripture—more than most modern "translations" do—and at the expense of Jesus.

The study was just the preliminary to the real purpose of the meetings: an exercise in which everyone was obligated to "spill his or her guts" in a series of glorified group therapy sessions. The aim of all this was, of course, to make everyone feel obligated to conform. The old peer pressure technique provided the needed leverage. Admittedly, all this gave some people a warm glow of intimacy and belonging that comes when personal interaction is of primary importance and sound doctrine is of little consequence.

I attended several sessions, so I can say that my impressions are not founded on just an isolated instance.

Thanks for unmasking this dangerous movement which is targeting those who have not developed their spiritual defenses. Unfortunately, this constitutes the majority of Christians, which explains the phenomenal growth of the purpose driven church.

Kindest regards,

B.R. / Omaha, Nebraska

Dear Noah:

Thank you so very much for the absolutely beautiful CD that your daughter did! We had wanted to order it when we received the newsletter, but felt we needed the book about the paganization of Christian music since our church is really going through the PDC struggles. We intend to pass the book around to the adults in Tom's Sunday school class. Thank you for having such excellent resource materials to help us.

By a lot of prayer and a lot of letters to our pastor, he has changed his mind about the modernization business and hopefully Rick Warren's stuff also. Talked Sunday night about the importance of expository preaching of God's Word. Hallelujah! You helped saved one church and, we trust, MANY!

We love you, thanks again.

T.G.

Dear Dr. Hutchings:

My family and I were so pleased to hear you and Dr. Spargimino at the Prophecy Conference in Anaheim last month. It was a great blessing. It was also a great blessing to see so many turn out for the event, especially in view of the fact that this conference was being held in such close physical proximity to the Saddleback Church (and its false teachings) to the south. We are grateful for you and Dr. Bob

Glaze and all the other speakers for coming to this conference.

I do admire, though, your stand against Rick Warren and against so many other errors. We would therefore like to start supporting your ministry on a quarterly basis. There are just so few organizations and men willing to take a stand for Christ these days. We are therefore glad to see you and Southwest Radio Church are doing so.

Love in Christ,

C.H.

Dear Brother Hutchings:

We have recently left our church of fourteen years because the *Purpose Driven Life* was chosen to be studied in all home group meetings. We had just ordered *Who Is Driving the Purpose Driven Church?* and also *Deceived On Purpose.* We went to our senior pastor and protested the use of Dr. Warren's material. We gave the two books we had read, plus some material from Twin Cities Fellowship which we found on the Internet. The pastor promised to study the "anti-purpose driven" material but after three weeks he had not read anything. We were just "brushed off." We had been the head of our congregation intercessory prayer ministry for fourteen years. I believe we are seeing the great apostasy of the end-times.

Sincerely,

B.C.

Dear Brother Hutchings:

I had to write you after we read your last *Prophetic Observer* on these PDC churches. We are living in the last days, I believe. These churches bringing in this music trying to get young people into church is of the devil himself.

Why are churches going so liberal?

Mrs. P.C.

Dear Dr. Hutchings:

Thank you so much for your input regarding the purpose driven church movement. . . .

Enclosed is a copy of my letter of resignation and I thank you again for alerting me concerning this issue:

Dear Friends:

My heart is sorely grieved that I am compelled to write this letter. Worship is being diminished with the purpose driven church growth movement creeping into ---------- (i.e., Rick Warren/Kent Hunter). One cannot follow a market driven strategy and remain faithful to Scripture.

God's Word in Romans 12:2 says: "And be not conformed to this world: but be ye transformed by the renewing of your mind, that ye may prove what is that good, and acceptable, and perfect, will of God." Also, 1 John 2:15 states: "Love not the world, neither the things that are in the world. If any man love the world, the love of the Father is not in him." In Acts 5:29 we read: "Then Peter and the other apostles answered and said, We ought to obey God rather than men."

*The true church is for Christians and is a rescue mission for lost souls. A soul will only realize God's blessings through God-centered biblical preaching which is **sin-exposing, self-convicting,** and **life-challenging.** No other means will bring a person to Christ, as is so specifically quoted in John 14:6: "Jesus saith unto him, I am the way, the truth, and the life: no man cometh unto the Father, but by me."*

Because of these facts, I cannot, with a clear conscience, continue to serve my Lord at ---------- when Jesus Christ is being driven out and replaced with a New Age, self-esteem, "feel good" gospel! I pray that the membership of ---------- will not be deceived by this apostate marketing ploy currently being introduced into the churches via books written by Rick Warren, which are The Purpose Driven Church *and* The Purpose Driven Life, *as well as Robert Schuller's* Mountain Moving

Faith *and* The New Reformation, *all of which are very dangerous since they promote evil and* **do not** *tell people they are sinners.* **The purpose driven movement is preparing Christendom to give its allegiance to someone other than the God of Scripture.** *Romans 1:16 states: "For I am not ashamed of the gospel of Christ: for it is the power of God unto salvation to every one that believeth. . . ." I will* **not** *compromise. I will stay true to the Gospel of my Lord and Saviour, Jesus Christ.*

For the above reasons, I am left no choice but to resign as organist from ----------, effective June 5, 2005.

I love and will miss each of you, and will continually keep you in my prayers.

Love,

E.N. / Michigan

Chapter 7

Music With a Purpose

Dr. Rick Warren was asked by a newspaper reporter: "If you weren't a pastor, what would you have been?"

Dr. Warren replied:

> A rock musician, probably. Growing up, I played guitar. I had shoulder-length, blonde hair. I was interested in government. But you don't change society through laws. You do it through individual lives. If you want to affect culture, you have to start with people's hearts and lives.
>
> —*Dallas Morning News,* May 20, 2005

Dr. Warren evidently lost his long, blonde hair since the '60s, but not his love for the hippie music of that generation. One aspect of that lifestyle that Dr. Warren evidently did not change was his love for rock music. Rock music is a vital part of the purpose driven church movement. The five senses of the human being as a composite soul are interdependent. Something that smells bad also may make you sick at your stomach. Something that appears ugly and gruesome may make you angry or despondent. Listening to different types of music also influences attitudes and personalities. The type of music, whether in the church or outside the church, indicates whether men and women may be worshipping God or entertaining secular or erotic behavior or ideas. Moses knew what the Hebrews were doing during his forty days of absence before he got to camp. He heard their singing and music from a distance and knew what they were doing—engaging in a sexual orgy involving the majority of the camp. Nebuchadnezzar knew that if he played a loud and certain kind of music that the masses would fall down and worship anything . . . even him.

Dr. Warren's mission is to change the church from a traditional New Testament model to a contemporary, or a 1960s, young, "flower generation" model. This is why he said to get rid of the old pillars and play a certain type of rock music. One of the first items in the transition agenda is to get rid of the choir and the organ, and to play loud rock music. At my former church, the minister of music indicated that the efforts to bring the new PDC pastor predated his appearance by two years. And, "coincidentally," the music at my church began to change two years before he was "called" by the "search" committee.

In World War II before I went to the South Pacific war arena, my unit was sent to Fort Ord, California, for Ranger training. Too many soldiers were not physically fit to stand the hardships, having mental breakdowns, or turning tail under fire. In Ranger training we were subjected to six weeks of the most brutal physical and mental training possible. At the end of the six weeks, when an officer said halt, we stopped; jump, we jumped; fight, we fought. Every command was obeyed without thought. We didn't care whether we lived or died; obedience was more important than life. But one of the most important parts of the training was the music. From 5:30 a.m. until 10:00 p.m. when we were in camp, harsh military band music blared over the loud speakers. I can hear the drums: step-step-step-step-step—run-run-run-run-run-yell-yell-yell-yell-yell . . .

Dr. Jack Wheaton, Emmy Award winner and professor of music at three major universities, including the University of Southern

California, and lecturer at over fifty colleges, wrote in his book *The Paganization of Worship:*

> It's happening. We are being spiritually and morally deceived by allowing Christian rock to become part of our worship service. In fact, in some churches today, it is the most important part, particularly if liberal pastors and churches read and believe their own propaganda, that the "unsaved" will not set foot in a church without it being filled with satanically-inspired music. It's like a bad dream.

Pioneers

"What we dish out is the musical equivalent of war—war upon quiet, war upon dullness, war upon certainty and stability" (The Who, interview in *Rolling Stone*, Vol. 2).

The major innovators and pioneers came mostly from Great Britain, with the Beatles and the Rolling Stones being the two strongest European forces in early rock music. The Stones are still performing, even though several are grandfathers today. The Rolling Stones began as a cover group for the cuddly Beatles. With a new manager, they changed their persona and now set out to "free" teenagers from cultural restrictions and to irritate parents:

"Rock music is sex, and you have to hit them in the face with it!" (Mick Jagger of the Rolling Stones, taken from *The Satan-Seller* by Mike Warnke, 1972).

Sex, Drugs and Rock

"If exposed long enough to the tom-toms [drums] and the singing, every one of our philosophers would end by capering and howling with the savages.... Assemble a mob of men and women previously conditioned by a daily reading of newspapers, treat them to amplified band music, bright lights . . . and in next to no time you can reduce them to a state of almost mindless subhumanity. Never before have so few been in a position to make fools, maniacs, or criminals of so many" (Aldous Huxley, *The Devils of Loudun,* 1952).

The above was the battle cry of the culture-rebellious hippies of the '60s. Today the musical style of rock and its billions of fans are just as closely tied to this motto as ever:

"'In rock, you're supposed to outrageous,' says Lou Cox, a New York-based psychologist who specializes in addictions. 'Being bad is good. The culture is not only supportive of addiction,' he continues, 'it's as if there is a demand for it—like it's part of the credibility package'" (Michael Paeoletta, *San Diego Union–Tribune*).

Addictive?

The primary reason for the power and popularity of rock music is the fact that it can be addictive. I'm not talking just about "liking" the music, I am talking about a physical addiction. Rock music rediscovered the power of pagan music in its volume, repetitiveness, and highly syncopated rhythm patterns. Loud rock music triggers the fight-or-flight response, initiates the first stages of hypnosis, and overcomes conscious resistance to becoming part of a group consciousness. Detoxing from rock music can be just as difficult as detoxing from cigarettes, alcohol, or so-called recreational drugs. Many in both the secular and so-called Christian rock community had to struggle to detox from this music.

Early Death

The average life expectancy of a full-fledged rock 'n roller is around forty years. So many of the greats checked out early: from Jim Morrison of the Doors, Keith Moon of the Who, Sid Vicious of the Sex Pistols, Jimi Hendrix, Janis Joplin, and Brian Jones of the Rolling Stones, to contemporary artists such as Bradley Nowell of Sublime, Shannon Hoon of Blind Melon, and Kurt Cobain of Nirvana.

There is a growing awareness that death is nature's way of telling you to slow down, as well as the economic reality that dead artists can't sell records . . . and benefit from it. Recent superstars like Whitney Houston, Courtney Love, Natalie Cole, Ozzy Osbourne, Mary J. Blige, Anthony Kiedis of the Red Hot Chili Peppers, Michael Jackson, and Dr. John represent just a partial list of those who have admitted addiction and have submitted to professional treatment.

"In the mid 1980s Aerosmith broke down the door that made it okay for big-name artists to go public with their sobriety, according to industry observers. In the years since, Eric Clapton, Boy George, Bonnie Raitt, James Taylor, Elton John, and others have all made their sobriety known" (Michael Paeoletta, *San Diego Union–Tribune*).

Is There Something in the Music?

"The loud sounds and the bright lights of today are tremendous indoctrination tools" (Frank Zappa, of Mothers of Invention, quoted from "Music in Education Today," by D. L. Cuddy, *Union–Leader* [NH]).

The fact that so many of the leading rock artists are addicted to drugs or alcohol or have died from overdoses, along with a very high percentage of their fans, can't help but make one wonder if there is something in the music itself that contributes to this plague.

"The big beat [rock] is deliberately aimed at exciting the listener. There is actually very little melody, only rhythm. . . . We seem to be reverting to savagery. . . . Youngsters who listen constantly to this sort of sound are thrust into turmoil. They are no longer relaxed, normal kids" (Dimitri Tiomkin, Academy Award-winning film composer, quoted from "Music in Education Today," by D. L. Cuddy).

I believe there is something in the music that contributes heavily to drug addiction. First, the volume itself, along with the sharp after-beat of the drums, triggers the fight-or-flight response, causing the body to self-medicate itself via the brain to the adrenal glands. Secondly, I believe the anarchistic lyrics promote drug use, sexual promiscuity, and social rebellion. The costumes alone tell us that these are not normal human beings on stage.

Negative Physiological Effects

Dr. John Diamond, a New York City psychiatrist, studied rhythmic beats of over twenty thousand recordings and concluded:

"A specific beat (stopped anapestic rhythm, which is contrary to our natural body beats and rhythms) found in over half of the top hits of any given week can actually weaken you.... It interferes with brain wave patterns, causing mental stress. Tests conducted in schools showed that students performed 15 percent better without rock music" ("Music in Education Today," by D. L. Cuddy).

Study after study is increasingly showing the physiological and mental damage that can be self-inflicted on a teenager through rock music. Hearing loss is a major complaint, and former president Bill Clinton, although still a relatively young man, had to be fitted for hearing aids five years ago. He blamed his hearing loss on listening to loud rock music while growing up in Arkansas.

How About the Brain?

The human brain is the most marvelous biocomputer ever invented. All modern-day computers are modeled after the human brain. None have ever come close to duplicating its incredible abilities. However, the brain is delicate. Sudden, threatening changes in the environment (loud sounds), or dangerous chemicals (drugs, alcohol), or hypnotic stages can alter the brain permanently.

"'Snapping' depicts the way in which intense experience may affect fundamental information-processing capacities of the brain. The [negative] experience itself may ... render the individual extremely vulnerable to suggestion. It may lead to changes that alter lifelong habits, values, and belief systems" (Flo Conway and Jim Siegelman: *America's Epidemic of Sudden Personality Change,* 1978).

—Dr. Jack Wheaton, *Crisis in Christian Music:*
The Paganization of Worship, Vol. 2, ©2004

Purple Haze with a Purpose?

The Assist News Service (ANS) carried a story of Dr. Rick Warren's annual super-meeting held this year at the Anaheim Angels' baseball stadium, with a reported thirty thousand in attendance. The story was headlined, "Rick Warren Hits Home Run with Announcement of Global Peace Plan to Battle the Giants of Our World."

Dr. Warren announced at this meeting in Anaheim "his" plan to send one billion church members into the world to eliminate hunger, disease, crime, and war. When he revealed his P.E.A.C.E. plan calling for global Christianity, Dr. Warren stated, "I'm looking at a stadium full of people who are telling God they will do whatever it takes to establish God's kingdom on earth as it is in heaven."

We read in Daniel 2:44–45 that a "great stone" will strike the last of the world gentile empires, bash it into small pieces, and then fill the whole world and "set up a kingdom" of the "God of heaven" that will "never be destroyed." Peter and Paul indicate that the "rock" of Daniel 2 is Jesus Christ at His Second Coming (Rev. 19). Maybe Erasmus or Tyndale made a mistake in translating. Maybe the original documents read, "Dr. Warren will set up the kingdom of heaven that will never be destroyed."

When Dr. Warren puts his "peace" plan into operation, then the world will know peace and the "kingdom of heaven" will be on earth and God's will will be done on earth as it is in Heaven. The ANS report continued:

> But before he made the announcement, he decided to have some fun and surprise the audience when he said, "I've always wanted

to do this in this stadium." He then sang an impersonation of Jimi Hendrix's hit song, "Purple Haze." As the audience erupted into laughter, the church band joined in playing back up to it.

The drug LSD became popular with the hippie, free-love, drop-out generation of the '60s. After taking it, inanimate objects and plants became animated walking and talking companions, with the earth and sky putting on a hazy, purple mantle. Jimi Hendrix, a black guitar player, connected his metal guitar to an electric amplifier and the heavy metal sound was added to the "rock music" sounds of Elvis and the Beatles. Jimi Hendrix became the idol of the pot-immersed, drug-soaked, mind-blown, sex-crazed new youth rebellion generation. Those who have Internet capability can pull up the Jimi Hendrix web site. There you will find that he was continually stoned on pot or doped up on various drugs, including heroin. It was not uncommon for him to have sex with six different women a day. His most famous song was "Purple Haze," probably written while on LSD. Following are the lyrics to the song:

Purple haze all in my brain
Lately things just don't seem the same
Actin' funny, but I don't know why
'Scuse me while I kiss the sky
Purple haze all around
Don't know if I'm comin' up or down
Am I happy or in misery?
Whatever it is that girl put a spell on me

Purple haze all in my eyes
Don't know if it's day or night
You got me blowin', blowin' my mind
Is it tomorrow, or just the end of time?

Jimi Hendrix died one day in 1970, drowning in his own vomit, from a heroin drug overdose.

The singing of "Purple Haze" by Dr. Rick Warren before thirty thousand in the Angels' stadium to prelude his one billion-man peace plan was no accident. He said that he had always wanted to do this. It was planned, because his own church band had the music and were prepared to accompany him. Is this the type of "Christian music" the Saddleback Church members hear on Sunday morning? Dr. Warren has said of the music at Saddleback:

> At Saddleback we are unapologetically contemporary.... And right after we made that decision and stopped trying to place everybody, Saddleback exploded with growth.... We are loud. We are really, really loud.... We're not gonna turn it down.... Baby boomers want to feel the music, not just hear it.
> —"Selecting Worship Music," by R. Warren, July 29, 2002

In introducing his world peace crusade, why would Dr. Warren memorialize the one person who was probably more responsible for turning America's youth to drugs, rebellion, and sex than any other? Chuck Colson, Dr. Billy Graham, and President Bush, according to ANS, sent prayers, greetings, and best wishes to Dr. Warren on the occasion.

> Let the word of Christ dwell in you richly in all wisdom; teaching and admonishing one another in psalms and hymns and spiritual songs, singing with grace in your hearts to the Lord. And whatsoever ye do in word or deed, do all in the name of the Lord Jesus, giving thanks to God and the Father by him
> —Colossians 3:16–17

The singing of hymns and the psalms appears to have been an important part of the early church services (Eph. 5:19). I doubt that "Purple

Haze" was in the early church hymn books.

I would doubt that the purpose driven church movement would have ever gotten off the ground without the heavy-metal rock, drug-inspired, hippie music of the '60s that has been revived by a new champion in so-called church praise groups. This music came out of one of the darkest period of national morality, the 1960s hippie generation, so need we say more.

Chapter 8

Follow the Dollar, Euro, Yuan, Shekel, Franc, Mark, Yen, Lira, Peso, Etc.

It is no one's business how much money a prostitute may have, or what she may do with her money. However, it is society's business, and civil authorities' concern, as to how she got her money.

Dr. Rick Warren doubtless has a lot of money. It is no one's business, except perhaps that of the IRS, as to how much money Dr. Warren has or what he does with his money. However, if he has made his money by prostituting the Gospel of Jesus Christ, then it is a matter of serious concern for the church universal, and individual Christians as well.

Since I was a teenager on the farm I had always heard the expression, "Holy Toledo." I always thought perhaps there must be a lot of churches in Toledo, Ohio. Several years ago, while on a mission tour to Africa and the Middle East, I stopped over in Madrid, Spain, where I learned there was another Toledo—Toledo, Spain. This was the real Holy Toledo and being only fifty miles from Madrid, I decided to find out what was so holy about Toledo. The city was completely surrounded by a high wall, and it had been the capital of Catholicism in Spain during the time of the Spanish Inquisition. Inside the city was a huge Catholic cathedral. In the circuit of the inside wall of the cathedral were glass display units containing huge idols of the Virgin Mary and the saints made of gold and precious gems worth millions or billions of dollars. Spanish explorers had sent back to the church their plunder of Mexico and the New World, where it evidently ended up at Toledo. As I walked through the cathedral, I thought of the description of the great whore in Revelation 17:4–5:

> And the woman was arrayed in purple and scarlet colour, and decked with gold and precious stones and pearls, having a golden cup in her hand full of abominations and filthiness of her fornication: And upon her forehead was a name written, MYSTERY, BABYLON THE GREAT, THE MOTHER OF HARLOTS AND ABOMINATIONS OF THE EARTH.

Not only the Catholic Church is guilty of spiritual prostitution in using the Gospel to collect the wealth of the world, but today Protestant churches and non-Catholic churches own properties worth untold billions of dollars. The Separation of Church and State Organization in Washington, D.C., lists church-owned properties from distilleries to truck companies to ranches to night clubs. It is not uncommon for pastors, ministers, and evangelists to own homes worth millions of dollars. The apostle Paul set for us an example for ministers to follow:

> Neither did we eat any man's bread for nought; but wrought with labour and travail night and day, that we might not be chargeable to any of you: Not because we have not power, but to make ourselves an ensample unto you to follow us.
>
> 2 Thessalonians 3:8–9

This does not mean that pastors and ministers have to work at McDonalds or wash dishes at the local beanery. It does mean keeping a humble material image. The most often mentioned sins of the clergy in the Bible are hypocrisy, worldliness, blasphemy, apostasy, and spiritual fornication, using the Kingdom of God as a means to build their own material kingdom here on earth.

Referencing an article by Dr. Gary E. Gilley, "The Gospel According to Warren" (*www.svchapel.org*), we read:

> No one has exemplified the market-driven approach better than Rick Warren, pastor of the huge Saddleback Church in southern California and author of *The Purpose-Driven Church* and *The Purpose-Driven Life*. While Warren is open and up-front about his philosophy, strategy and methods, nevertheless things are not always as they appear. For example, "purpose-driven" sounds better than "market-driven" but it is basically the same thing. In his book *The Purpose-Driven Life,* his opening statement is, "It is not about you," then turns around and writes a whole book about "you." He belittles pop-psychology then repeatedly promotes it by simply calling it something else. He publicly cuts ties with Robert Schuller, then regurgitates some of the most odious things that Schuller has been teaching for thirty years. He claims commitment to the Scriptures then undermines them at almost every turn. He will tell his followers that he is not tampering with the message but only reengineering the methods, when in fact he has so altered the message as to make it all but unrecognizable.

One of the largest publishers of books on Christian or other religious themes is Zondervan Publishing Company, once owned by the Zondervan family. Zondervan published a book I wrote back in the 1960s. When Pat Zondervan, the president of the company died, the company was sold to Rupert Murdoch.

Zondervan Publishing Company published Dr. Warren's books *The Purpose Driven Church* and *The Purpose Driven Life.* The sales reported a year ago was over twenty million copies. This number now probably exceeds thirty million. Zondervan is one of many companies owned by Australian billionaire Rupert Murdoch. Mr. Murdoch loves money and he has a lot of it. He also owns Harper/Collins, which publishes numerous magazines, one which advertised on its web site, March 9, 2005, "Sensational Single Women: Get the love and sex you deserve! Send your friends the link . . ." Mr. Murdoch also owns *The Sun* in England. You who have the Internet can click on *The Sun*, pull up page three, and see what kind of sleazy, sex-oriented newspaper it is. Some of Mr. Murdoch's publications and media outreaches have been rated between XX and XXX pornographic. It would seem evident that Mr. Murdoch does not publish Dr. Warren's books out of evangelistic concerns. With his many worldwide media advantages, it would seem evident the bigger he makes Dr. Warren, the more books he sells, and the richer he becomes.

Mr. Murdoch also owns Fox, a balanced, conservative TV news outlet to compete with CNN. However, this does not make Mr. Murdoch a conservative, just as publishing *The Purpose Driven Life* does not make him a Christian. The February 21, 2005, edition of the *London Daily Telegraph* was headlined, "Murdoch Poised for Chinese Television Joint Venture." The Telegraph Group Limited, on December 21, 2004, reported that Mr. Murdoch became a member of the China Netcom Board, and that he is building for his third wife, Chinese citizen Wendi Deng, who presently runs his Hong Kong "Star" pay-TV operation (which is morally questionable), a 22,000-foot underground home at the Forbidden City in Beijing. I was arrested in the Forbidden City and taken to jail for telling the Chinese that God loved them, and now Mr. Murdoch builds an underground palace there for his wife, a mover in Chinese economics and politics. I would have a problem of conscience with Mr. Murdoch publishing my books. Maybe Dr. Warren doesn't.

According to *Businessweek,* as reported in the July 16, 2004, Center for American Progress (*www.americanprogress.org*):

...his satellites deliver TV programs in five continents, all but dominating Britain, Italy, and wide swaths of Asia and the Middle East. He publishes 175 newspapers, including the *New York Post* and *The Times of London*. In the U.S., he owns the Twentieth Century Fox Studio, Fox Network, and 35 TV stations that reach more than 40 percent of the country.... His cable channels include fast-growing Fox News, and 19 regional sports channels. In all, as many as one in five American homes at any given time will be turned into a show News Corp. either produced or delivered.

Mr. Murdoch became a U.S. citizen in 1985 and over the Fox news network presents a conservative and patriotic image, evidently for profit, because overseas he is a political pragmatist for profit. According to *Time* magazine, from the previously noted Center of American Progress report, Mr. Murdoch cancelled BBC over his Star TV system for showing the 1989 massacre of Chinese students on Tiananmen Square. James Murdoch, his son, also labeled the Falun Gong as a dangerous, apocalyptic cult, and applauded the Chinese government's effort to eliminate the Falun Gong movement. Due to the manipulation of his multi-company stocks between his many foreign-owned companies, according to BBC, he pays only a 6 percent tax on excess profits, while most other large companies pay between 31 and 36 percent.

While Zondervan still publishes some of the traditional titles, like the books by Dr. Herbert Lockyer and the *Kids KJV Study Bible,* most of its efforts now are directed toward the publishing of purpose driven church books by Dr. Rick Warren. At twenty dollars a book, thirty million books would amount to $600 million. Having written a number of books myself, I would estimate that Dr. Warren receives about two dollars a book royalty. Thirty million books would thus result in $60 million royalty, a nice piece of change. I qualify this estimate by saying again this is based on my experience, and that I am not privy to any royalty agreement between Zondervan and Dr. Warren.

He could receive more, he could receive less.

Some may wonder if with me this is not just another case of the pot calling the kettle black. I live in a house my wife and I bought on a ten-year mortgage for $48,000 in 1988, and have since added on a 10′ x 10′ catch-all building. I have been with this organization for fifty-four years, and at least half the staff receive more than I do in wages. I would estimate that about thirty thousand of my books are distributed through the ministry each year, for which I receive six thousand dollars a year in royalties to offset my own expenses, and I think I am the most God-blessed man in the world. I have in good conscience tried to follow Paul's example, and although I may not have followed it perfectly, I still follow after.

Returning to the affiliation and fellowship between Mr. Murdoch and Dr. Warren, in England, the United States, and Australia, Mr. Murdoch presents himself as a nationalist. This could possibly also include China as a result of his marriage to a Chinese citizen. However, in international economics he is a political pragmatist and a New World Order advocate. Dr. Rick Warren seems to be in agreement, as we might expect. Whoever pays the piper calls the tune.

Quoting from the June 16, 2004, edition of the *Washington Post*:

> The Southern Baptist Convention voted yesterday to pull out of the Baptist World Alliance, accusing the worldwide organization of a drift toward liberalism that included growing tolerance of homosexuality, support for women in the clergy and "anti-American pronouncements."
>
> The Baptist World Alliance, which has a 20-member staff at its headquarters in Falls Church, is a loose, voluntary confederation of 211 Baptist groups with more than 46 million members around the globe.
>
> The Rev. Paige Patterson, president of the Southwestern Baptist

Theological Seminary, told yesterday's meeting that the alliance also contains "gay-friendly" churches that support same sex-marriage. "What you give your money and name to, you give tacit approval to," he said.

President Bush spoke to the gathering in Indianapolis yesterday via video link and reiterated his support for a constitutional amendment to ban gay marriage. It was the third year in a row that Bush has spoken to the Southern Baptists, and he urged them to lobby Congress to pass the amendment.

Now quoting from the July 28, 2005, edition of the *Biblical Recorder*:

Birmingham England—Affirming that Baptists from around the world can "have unity without uniformity," Rick Warren told reporters at the Baptist World Alliance's (BWA) centenary congress that the withdrawal of Southern Baptists from BWA was a "silly" mistake.

During a July 28 press conference, Warren addressed a question about last year's decision by the Southern Baptist Convention (SBC), the largest BWA member to withdraw membership and funding from BWA. "I think that was a mistake," he said flatly. "When the Southern Baptists pulled out funding, my wife and I wrote a check for $25,000 to BWA."

"The first Reformation was about beliefs. This one needs to be about behavior."

In response to their newfound fame and fortune, Warren said he and his wife, Kay, set up three foundations, including one to provide ministry to people with AIDS and one to help train pastors. He also stopped taking a salary from Saddleback and returned the salary the church had paid him the past 25 years.

In response, Warren has endorsed the One Campaign to reduce

world hunger and has unveiled a "PEACE plan" urging every local church to be involved in planting churches, fighting poverty and AIDS, and promoting education.

"Issues like disease and poverty and education I will work on with anybody," he said. "Those are not just Baptist issues. Those are human issues."

In referencing his objection of the Southern Baptists pulling out of the Baptist World Alliance, Dr. Warren also said, as reported in the *Biblical Recorder*, "I see absolutely zero reason in separating my fellowship from anybody." In his interview with the *Dallas Morning News* of May 16, 2005, Dr. Warren said in reference to his success, that he sticks closely to what the Bible says, "I quote over 1,500 Bible verses." Evidently Dr. Warren missed some: "And what concord hath Christ with Belial? or what part hath he that believeth with an infidel? . . . Wherefore come out from among them, and be ye separate, saith the Lord, and touch not the unclean thing; and I will receive you" (2 Cor. 6:15, 17).

What can we conclude about Dr. Warren's statements relating to the Baptist World Alliance:

1. He is following the Murdoch rationale while professing to be a conservative promoting a united world government.
2. He has no problem fellowshipping with those who are anti-American and pro-homosexual.
3. Changing the mission of the church from calling out of the gentiles a people for Christ's Name (Acts 15) to feed the poor, heal the sick, and bring peace on earth. This is secular humanistic charity, not evangelical Christianity.

Dr. Warren also contends that he is using the millions from the royalties from sale of his books to maintain his church, promote his billion-man peace army, humanitarian efforts abroad, and train some

400,000 in purpose driven church ministry. But this is simply taking money from one pocket and putting it in another. This is building up the kingdom of the purpose driven church, his own personal empire. The present denominations, and especially the Southern Baptist Convention, will wake up one morning and finally discover that they have a new pope.

And, as far as Dr. Warren giving back to his church twenty-five years of salary, plus unspecified amounts for his world peace venture, it is assumed that Saddleback is a 501(C)3 tax exempt entity. His royalties for the past couple of years would have been of such an amount that much of it would have been taken in IRS taxes anyway. So, then why not reduce the tax by giving part to his own mission and ministry, and then later the church can vote him a good salary at a much lower tax rate. Could it be he is taking some lessons in taxes from Mr. Murdoch?

But as we read in Daniel 2, the kingdoms of men come, and they go, even Rupert Murdoch's Camelot:

When News Corp. Chairman Rupert Murdoch married his third wife, Wendi Deng, in 1999, all four of his adult children attended the twilight ceremony aboard a yacht in the New York harbor. But since then, the marriage has opened a rift between Mr. Murdoch and his older children, one that throws into doubt who will control the company after the media titan's death.

The bitter battle has all the hallmarks of a classic family drama.

—*Wall Street Journal,* August 1, 2005

Jesus Christ the same yesterday, and to day, and for ever. Be not carried about with divers and strange doctrines. . . .

—Hebrews 13:8–9

Chapter 9

All Glory To Whom?

PDC Endorsers

An article that appeared in the February 2, 2005, edition of the *Baptist Messenger* by Pastor Alan Day of Edmond, Oklahoma, questioned mine, or anyone's right to criticize Dr. Warren or the purpose driven church movement when men like Dr. W. A. Criswell, Dr. Jerry Falwell, and others (I might add Dr. Billy Graham), are commending and endorsing him. Dr. Criswell did indeed write a glowing commendation of Dr. Warren in the introduction of Dr. Warren's book, *The Purpose Driven Church*. In *The Purpose Driven Church* Dr. Warren warns, however, that his program could meet with disaster when tried in other areas. This qualification was changed subsequently on his web site and promotional materials to warn churches that if they did not change to a PDC in five years, they probably would not be around. We would also wonder what Dr. Criswell would say today if he were alive, as the Criswell Center is being torn down to build a $55 million PDC social center.

Dr. Falwell did have Dr. Warren speak at two super–conferences in Lynchburg, because this helped add another few thousand registrants at four hundred dollars each. However, Dr. Falwell did not change his church to a purpose driven church format, because he knew if he did that half his congregation would walk. Dr. Billy Graham in his old age has become so ecumenized that he thinks the Mormon Church is a great Christian organization, and the late pope was the foremost ecclesiastical leader in the world. The Church Growth phenomenon seems to have congealed in the cultic adoration of one leader, Dr. Rick Warren. As in the internationally televised adoration of the late pope, John Paul II, worldwide communications make possible mass propaganda of intensified devotional attention to a single individual. The world today is being made ready for its own messiah in much the same way churches are being changed to places that the world accepts rather than the institution that God has sanctified.

I received the following letter from Pauline of Martinsville, Virginia, dated May 8, 2005:

Dear Noah Hutchings:

I read with much interest your article in your *Prophetic Observer* concerning Rick Warren and his purpose driven program.

I know you know God's Word so well. As I read this article, I feel so very worried that well-meaning Christian people can let themselves be led away by any wolf in sheep's clothing. . . . The Devil took one-third of the angels when he was thrown out of Heaven. There are always going to be people who aren't grounded in God's Word who can be led astray. But please, Mr. Hutchings, be kind to our brother in Christ, Billy Graham. This man has spent his adult life witnessing and preaching God's Word. This man has kept his personal opinion of his political beliefs out of his preaching. He has faithfully proclaimed God's Word. He has drawn millions to God by just that. He is only human, as you and I are. . . . I think Billy Graham is a wonderful human being. . . .

Pauline continued for another page recalling the extent of Dr. Graham's ministry over the past sixty years. I responded:

Dear Pauline:

Thanks for your letter we received May 12.

You are marvelous in your defense of an old lion who has lost strength, will, and courage to defend his territory and pride. It is not the man himself and his great ministry over the past sixty years that are in question, but those who now use his words and reputation to promote their own agenda.

If I ever need a champion to stand for me, I will keep you in mind. Thanks for your good advice, and God bless you for that. You are a most compassionate and gracious lady.

Faithfully yours,

Noah W. Hutchings

For the past twenty-five years I have annually written and produced a prophecy calendar on a mission basis for untold millions of prison cells around the world. In each calendar is the plan of salvation specially worded for inmates. We also send thousands of copies of our book *A Christian's Guide to Prison Survival,* and other books and videos, to chaplains for prison dissemination. On April 4, 2005, I received a letter from Yusuf in Kanater Men's Prison in Cairo, who wrote that he stayed up all night just to listen to our program. In the late '70s I communicated with David Berkowitz (the Son of Sam killer) while he was on trial. The district attorney of Queens subpoenaed the letters, but David was saved and is now serving out his life sentence as a chaplain's assistant at the prison in Fallsburg, New York. David's last letter to me, dated June 16, 2004, closed: "It will not be until you get to Heaven that you will know all those who were helped by your ministry. Keep the faith."

There are hundreds of prison mission efforts, many sponsored by local churches, doing a tremendous work for the Lord. Although the general public will never hear of these mission groups, God still gets the glory.

In April 2005 a distraught prison inmate on trial suddenly ran amok and killed a judge and several others in the courtroom. Afterward, the prisoner escaped and subsequently broke into an apartment occupied by a single woman in her mid-twenties. During the next twenty-four hours, the apartment occupant, Ms. Ashley Smith, at some point read to the escaped prisoner from Dr. Warren's *Purpose Driven Life* book, and also from the Bible, according to her pastor as reported to Fox and CNN. However, according to thousands of TV reports, newspaper, and magazine articles, Dr. Warren and his book were given 100 percent credit for the criminal suddenly surrendering to authorities. This resulted in additional millions of books being sold.

Now whether Brian Nichols, the man accused of this horrible crime, suddenly came to his senses, and to save himself realized that he must surrender to law enforcement officials, or whether he really was led to saving faith in Jesus Christ and gave himself up as a matter of conscience, only God knows. But, in this international news story that was disseminated to billions, did God get the glory, or did Dr. Warren? Without question, both Dr. Warren and Mr. Murdoch, moneywise, profited greatly.

According to a subsequent incident relating to the Ashley Smith story, a Mr. Thurman Billings of Madison, Wisconsin, tried to read *The Purpose Driven Life* to a burglar and the burglar responded by saying, "My purpose is to beat you up and steal your plasma TV." Mr. Billings did credit the hardback book with helping to fend off blows and injuring the burglar's fist. Zondervan, the publisher, issued a caution that trying to convert hardened criminals by reading from the book when a crime was being committed might not be the wisest thing to do (America Online, July 5, 2005).

However, for whatever ministry or outreach associated with the purpose driven church movement, the name of Rick Warren seems to be mentioned far more than Jesus Christ. So we have to wonder if in the purpose driven church there is enough glory for Dr. Warren and Jesus Christ both. I doubt it.

... Worthy is the Lamb that was slain to receive power, and riches, and wisdom, and strength, and honour, and glory, and blessing.

—Revelation 5:12

The following item of reference is a few sentences from Reform America's web site (*www.reformamerica.com*) titled **"A Purpose Driven Death"**:

Everyday on my way to work I see a gigantic billboard advertisement with the words, "Got purpose?" I am generally an optimistic person, but when I saw the billboard, I began to hang my head in shame. If we have to resort to ad campaigns and catchy slogans to get people to come into our modern day Kiwanis clubs we are in serious trouble.

I have been in two churches that have conducted the 40 Days of Purpose. I have read the book twice, been in a small group, completed the study guide, and watched the videos.

According to *pastors.com*, over 60,000 pastors subscribe to Rick Warren's Ministry Toolbox, a free weekly e-mail newsletter. However, with so many pastors using his materials, this is all the more reason for us to test everything according to the Holy Scriptures.

The Great Commission does not say, "Go ye therefore, and teach all nations, baptizing them in the name of the Father, the Son and the Holy Spirit: Teaching them to observe all things whatsoever Rick Warren has commanded you." There is no simple formula for revival. We all thought Mel Gibson's *Passion* would save America and be as big as the Second Coming, but we are still murdering 4,000 babies a day and are about to allow men to marry men in America. Either we repent of our compromised Christianity and cleverly packaged Christian Humanism or we will see persecution (God's method of church growth) come to America that will make *Foxe's Book of Martyrs* look like a children's book.

Friends, this is not a quick fix. We must rediscover the ancient pathways. We must first start by repenting in our own hearts and lives, and build our house on the Rock of Jesus Christ. We must build off the time tested methodologies from the Bible and not the latest New York Times Best Seller.

In addition to the 60,000 pastors mentioned in the above commentary, Dr. Warren himself has said he is training over 400,000 workers and plans to send one billion church members out on his world peace campaign.

I have communicated with hundreds over the past eighteen months who have left their church because of either *The Purpose Driven Life* taught as a special outreach effort, or becoming a full-blown PDC unit. Sometimes the departure is due to conscience, sometimes due to refusing to participate in a PDL study, or signing one of *The Purpose Driven Life* covenants or oaths. At other times the pastor, or the minister of music, will request the older and more conservative church members to leave just because they want unlimited freedom to initiate programs that Dr. Warren advises during the transition period. The following letter is from a couple in Hamilton, New Jersey:

Dear Brother Noah:

Well, Jim and I got the surprise of our lives. We have gone to our Baptist Church since the mid 1980s. We were informed that our membership, along with a deacon and his family and a couple of others were dropped. I asked why, and we were told that the church was going in a new direction and some people were holding it back.

I asked, do you mean the purpose driven church? He said, well … um, yes. But, if it were up to me I'd keep you. I replied, Thanks, but that is okay. . . . I talked with him about the purpose driven church, but it was like talking to a brick wall.

So we have no church. We've checked around to all other churches. They are all purpose driven, so we have a little service here at home. We have adopted Southwest Radio Church. I think the Lord is building up our faith to trust in Him only. Bless you as you remain his Watchmen on the Wall.

In Christ's Love,
Mr. & Mrs. J.G.P.

Covenants and Associates

The first covenant that Dr. Warren asks a potential purpose driven church member to make is titled, **"My Covenant,"** which he has already signed. He then asks the signer to get another partner, or witness, to sign, evidently to verify the signature and intention. This is a covenant that is made even before the buyer of the book has read the first page, so the signer does not yet know what he or she is really signing or swearing an oath to perform. But this first covenant is only the first of several covenants, including one that is a church loyalty oath or pledge binding the signer to the church leader and obedience to him and the church. Covenants were agreements between God and Israel, or between individuals, under the Law. The word "covenant" is found some 250 times in the Bible, 230 of these times in the Old Testament, usually referencing a contract between God and Israel. Most of the twenty times the word "covenant" is found in the New Testament refers back to Old Testament covenants. But Jesus Christ has made a new covenant that negates forever the need of covenants between God and man, and this is the covenant He made with His blood (Heb. 8:6; 13:20). So, why should Christians be asked to make a covenant with Dr. Warren or the purpose driven church?

Again, ye have heard that it hath been said by them of old time, Thou shalt not forswear thyself, but shalt perform unto the Lord thine oaths: But I say unto you, Swear not at all; neither by heaven; for it is God's throne: Nor by the earth; for it is his footstool: neither by Jerusalem; for it is the city of the great King. Neither shalt thou swear by thy head, because thou canst not make one hair white or black. But let your communication be, Yea, yea; Nay, nay: for whatsoever is **more than** these cometh of evil.

—Matthew 5:33-37

But above all things, my brethren, swear not, neither by heaven, neither by the earth, neither by any other oath: but let your yea be yea; and your nay, nay; lest ye fall into condemnation.

—James 5:12

Yet, many Christians are being forced out of their churches because they will not swear to or sign PDL covenants.

Dr. Warren has been accused by others of using the words of New Agers, psychologists, occultists, and mystic spiritists to emphasize or supplement his teachings. Certainly, in Dr. Warren's position it is easy to come into contact with those professionally that you might not agree with on matters of religion. However, Dr. Warren's verbiage in communicating with others at times on exceedingly important issues of Christian faith and doctrine is confusing. For example, the following is an exchange between CNN's Larry King and Dr. Rick Warren from a TV program of March 26, 2005:

KING: You can, though, Rick, have a purpose-driven life and be an agnostic or an atheist, can't you? Still do good, still help others, still have purpose?

WARREN: Absolutely, you can help other people. I believe that we were made for a purpose, and that purpose is really to know God and to serve God and to love God, and to serve other people by—serve God by serving others. You know, you can't really serve

God directly, Larry, not here on earth. The only way you can serve God is by serving other people.

KING: Since you believe in God, if an agnostic or an atheist is doing good, God appreciates it, according to you, right?

WARREN: God wants us all to be loving to each other, there is no doubt about that. In fact, Jesus wouldn't have made any distinction between someone who was of a different background. The issue was, do they love him and do they have a purpose? Are they following his purpose? See, I believe that we were made by God and that we were made for God. And that until we understand that, life isn't going to make sense. Now, really when it comes to . . .

As Jesus often did, when being interrogated by worldly wisdom, at times it is better to say nothing. As with Dr. Warren's response to Larry King, a true minister of God cannot be popular with the ungodly world and still faithful to the Lord Jesus Christ. If this is the kind of message that Dr. Warren plans to save the world with, then I think we should all pray:

Even so, come Lord Jesus!

Chapter 10

A Warning from a Concerned Parent and Youth Church Counselor

by Deborah Huestis

Following is the information I learned personally from being in two churches that accepted both the "Contagious Christian" program of Willow Creek and the "40 Days of Purpose" out of Saddleback, combined with some information from outside sources.

Two churches I have attended here in Great Falls had the exact same scenarios of structure change upon taking on the Contagious Christian and/or 40 Days of Purpose, including as follows:

1. Wednesday night "believer's service" removed.
2. In-church Bible studies (which, in both cases had been mostly precept studies) removed and combined with home fellowship, which was then renamed small groups, home groups, or cell groups.
3. Sunday sermons, as well as home group studies, carefully tailored to teach on bringing in the lost and serving the church.
4. Home groups were only allowed to use "Bible studies" that the

pastors either chose or prepared themselves, and always it lined up with whatever was presented on Sunday.

5. The Sunday sermons continually increased in what I call the entertainment factor: longer and more charismatic worship, sermons filled with more and more skits, video clips, and jokes, and more emphasis on the blessings of God rather than our obedience to His Word.

6. At some point a sermon series would be given on "fear" and at the next to the last week of the series a survey would be taken where everyone would fill in on a card what their greatest fear was. The next week the pastor would announce that the greatest fear was, "Not knowing your PURPOSE in life." This was when he would announce to the congregation that he had GREAT news! We do have a PURPOSE!!! He would then explain that for the next forty days the church would be reading a book that was to be considered a daily devotional and that it would change the lives of everyone in the church and give the church new life! (This, of course, was *The Purpose Driven Life*, and we were told that we would have the wonderful advantage of buying the book for half price if we bought it that day, in the church.) There are forty chapters and we were told that we were to read a chapter a day. As we left the sanctuary, everyone was handed a big button pin that said "40 Days of Purpose" in big letters with "I have a PURPOSE!" under it. We were also given key chains with the same thing written on the plastic-encased attachment.

7. At the end of the forty days, with the pastor basing all of his sermons on the book, of course, the entire church was instructed to come to a Saturday night simulcast where they would hear Rick Warren in person explain the program. (Which cost the church two thousand dollars just to show!) The people were enticed with a free dinner and sumptuous desserts.

8. At the end of the evening, everyone signed a *covenant* agreement

that they would, 1) stay committed to the program, and 2) *not cause division*. In other words, if they saw something down the road that seemed unscriptural to them, they *could not speak out!!!*

9. The next night was what they called the "ministry fair" where anyone who had a ministry of any kind could set up a "booth" and try to get people to sign up to help with it. At ---------- they had the ministry leaders (as well as the pastors themselves) dress up in old-fashioned baseball uniforms. They had baskets of peanuts on the counters beside the sign-up sheets and megaphones to get peoples' attention as they "bartered" for who was going to get talked into doing what! I heard it was literally like a circus!

10. I know that at ----------, the three "Bible studies" that the home groups can choose from are formatted (as in video format) by the worship leader/pastor. I suspect he receives his material from Saddleback and then uses himself to "teach" it through the video so that people will think it's his own stuff.

11. This, as is explained in the Gary E. Gilley book, *This Little Church Went to Market,* is not a short-term program. A former pastor of ---------- was let go two years ago because he could no longer agree with the long-term agenda of the above program. He told a woman who is a good friend of mine that the staff started receiving the material on how to "prepare" the congregation slowly for what would later be implemented, *at least three years* before the program was put in place! Upon addressing that issue when I had my "departure meeting" with the three remaining pastors last winter, I was told it had actually been *five!!!* (Does this remind you of the frog in the kettle?)

12. As you can hear, by listening to one of Rick Warren's interviews on the Hank Hanegraaff show, this is clearly a program of works, first to bring more people into the church and then to serve. Far more disturbing is the fact that it is carefully crafted to draw people out of the full counsel of God . . . first, by substituting as many

of the new translations as possible, second, by carefully dictating what they study, and, lastly, by keeping everyone so busy with the works that they feel that the time they spend in the word in their small groups is enough, therefore never learning the full counsel of God. Oh, and lest we forget, keeping them "happily entertained" and feeling "part of one big family"!! (The whole time signing one covenant after another.)

In summary, I have witnessed a very deliberate change of attitude and presentation of God in these churches. The concept of "fun" is presented first, over and over, increasing it steadily over time—both in worship and fellowship. I believe the "Contagious Christian" out of Willow Creek was created for that very purpose. When the people become used to the idea of church being "fun," the final hook and bait is thrown out, called "PURPOSE." Once they read the book *The Purpose Driven Life,* and agree that this is indeed the way they want to go as a church, the covenant signing begins and it's over.

I would like to address another facet of this program that concerns me greatly. For six years I was involved in several Christian-based programs in our public schools that were interdenominational. They were interactive with the different schools and churches, therefore giving me the opportunity to become acquainted with the youth pastors of most of the evangelical churches in our town. As the years passed, I began to notice a troubling pattern. As with the adult-level church services, the youth services were quickly becoming more and more entertainment-based. As one church would come up with a new "gimmick" to get the kids to come, the other churches would have to compete. Of the four largest youth groups, a black light was purchased by one for what they called "Black Light Friday Night." Therefore, soon one of the others bought a disco ball for their Friday night dances. The third started taking their kids to "Christian concerts" all over the state where there were mosh-pits, ear-shattering volume, and a total lack of dress codes. The fourth one started bringing in skateboarders, pro wrestlers, etc. (some brandishing tattoos and/or piercings), who claimed to be Christians but whose extreme lifestyles were fuel for rebellion.

In "Youth Alive," an in-school youth group of mostly churched kids, we would have a different youth pastor each month come to give a message. By the spring of my sixth year I made the conscious decision to break the rules by eliminating the youth pastors for the rest of the year. I could no longer listen to their skit- and joke-filled, Scripture-void "messages" while watching the kids look and act no differently than the rest of the kids in school. I decided that for the short time I had left I would show these students what God's Word had to say about the witchcraft many of them were practicing (thanks to the "Harry Potter" books), the piercings and tattoos more and more of them were getting, and the sensual way many of them were dressing and behaving. I started showing them the Ten Commandments (of which not one out of seventy knew) and ended by showing them Galatians 5:19–20. Needless to say, they were shocked—and I was given "the boot"! Hopefully, some of those seeds found fertile ground.

In the same year, I observed an even more concerning development that went side-by-side with the increase of entertainment and the lack of correction. The focus, in both worship and prayer, became more charismatic and experiential. The days of memorizing and studying Scripture exponentially were being replaced with a few carefully selected scriptures to go along with a super-charged time of worship and prayer that became the new social experience of choice for more and more kids. Here's my concern . . . We know that one of the goals of the purpose driven movement is to bring Eastern meditation into the church in the camouflaged name of "contemplative prayer." Meditation is one of the highest forms of pagan, altered-mind practices in the world, and God's Word absolutely forbids it. The root of meditation is found in Hinduism, probably going back to Babylon. But, it is also practiced by the Buddhists, New Agers, and even some sects of Islam.

In fact, there is probably no pagan religion in the world that does not practice this repetition-based, altered state-of-mind exercise, in one form or another. In Exodus 23:20–24 God forbids his children to do anything "according to the works" (practices) of the pagan nations He was sending them into. He told them He would defeat their enemies if they obeyed Him, but that they would be the defeated ones if they did not. In Matthew 6:7 Jesus warned His disciples not to use "vain repetitions, as the heathen do" when they prayed. Clearly this pagan practice is forbidden, but the problem is that more and more of the churched youth are Bible illiterate. God gives us a clear warning of living in this state of ignorance in Hosea 4:6: "My people are destroyed for lack of knowledge. . . ."

As our precious youth are led further and further into the entertainment/experiential spirituality and away from the truth and obedience of God's Word, they are, at the same time, being told that they will be able to connect with God in a *new way* . . . that they will be the generation to see God's Spirit poured out like never before. They use a misinterpretation of Joel 2:28–29 to promote this. This passage of scripture does indeed refer to a time when God will pour His Spirit out like never before. It says, ". . . Your sons and your daughters shall prophesy, your old men shall dream dreams, your young men shall see visions." But it will not be done through a pagan practice—in fact, just the opposite. But what young person would not want to be one of these end-time prophets? What young person would not want to hear God in a "new way" and be filled with the Holy Spirit like never before? Lastly, what young person wouldn't trust their youth pastor if he told them that there was a way to do that—a way practiced long ago by the "ancient desert fathers"?

I have watched the beginning of this movement come into our youth groups and my heart breaks at the gullibility of the youth and the apathy of the adults to take a stand against it. With our culture being so open now to Eastern practices (yoga, karate, etc.) I fear that this cleverly disguised practice of meditation will come in like a flood very soon and one of the last barriers between "us" and "them" (Christians and heathens) will be removed. Satan will then have an awesome and fearful tool with which to deceive and destroy our youth. Ray Youngen has written an excellent book on the subject *A Time of Departing* that I feel is an absolute must read, and the sooner the better! I pray that God will open the eyes of many adults to this book so that they can then speak out to other adults and, together, try to stop this cancer from infecting our youth. Ezekiel says that we are to be a watchman when we see the sword coming, or the blood of those taken by the sword will be on our hands. If we love your youth, we must speak out!!

Chapter 11

As the World Squirms, Quo Vadis PDC

The time-worn radio and TV soap series "As the World Turns" kept its character actors in a constant state of personal uncertainties and conflicts to hold the continuing interest of hearers or viewers to maintain a consistent audience and sell more detergents. The borrowing of a similar wording of this household drama is because the situations portrayed in the series reminds us of the daily changing international uncertainties of the world today.

A madman in Iran threatens to erase Israel and the United States off the map; the Association of Atomic Scientists has moved the doomsday clock to five minutes until midnight; global warming theorists predict that half the existing land mass will soon be under water; gas is expected to go to at least ten dollars a gallon; al Queda and other Islamic terrorists threaten to kill everyone who is not a Muslim, and tragedies like the Virginia Tech massacre are sure to increase in number and victims. Yet, if we pre-mil ministers mention that these could be warning signs of the time of trouble and tribulation such as the world has never seen before, we are called escapists or doomsdayers. However, in view of this evidently increasing world crisis, where does the remaining ninety-five percent of the non-Catholic church membership stand? What is their view of the future?

This past month I received a notice related to a conference in Asheville, North Carolina, titled "The 2007 Worldview Super Conference." Some of the speakers listed were Gary DeMar, Hank Hanegraaff, Gary North, Hugh Ross, and others. The conference would present the replacement theology of the Catholic Church, Constantine, and Augustine, that the church is going to bring in the Kingdom of Heaven, and then perhaps, invite Jesus to come back. This was the flawed eschatology that the Protestant denominations never gave up after A.D. 1500 (Presbyterian, Lutheran, Anglican, etc.). Part of the promotional material stated in part:

> The Church has been paralyzed by an obsession with life in the Last Days and lost sight of fulfilling the Great Commission to teach the nations to obey all of Christ's commandments.... America's restoration will lead to a more stable social structure, a prosperous economy, and a happier nation—demonstrating to the world the blessings and glory of living in a truly Christian nation … as well as build Christian nations around the world. Can it be done? Absolutely."

This traditional worldview of the A-mil/post-mil, rose-colored glasses theologians, is also that of Dr. Sproul, Dr. Kennedy, and others. The world as it will be in the last days, as prophesied by Daniel and Jesus, is a time of tribulation such as never was before or never would be again. That world to the A-mils will never exist. However, if the church is going to bring in the Kingdom and make the nations, including our own, such a wonderful place, why did Jesus go to prepare another place for us? Why take us out of the world (1 Thess. 4:13–18)? Why not just give us glorified bodies and leave us here?

While I would certainly disagree with the positional eschatology of the preceding theologians, at least their intentions to make all nations Christian is commendable, if not realistic or prophetically accurate. What should be of more serious concern, however, to fundamental ministers and memberships today are those who would expand the A-mil/post-mil illusion to include all religions.

Dr. Rick Warren is given credit for starting the purpose driven church movement. He devised and initiated a new church growth movement that made the church more like the world, with secular type entertainment to tempt the unchurched to attend church. This format would provide a situation where Hell was not mentioned and sin was no more sin. The unchurched could attend church and feel like a Christian without a change in their spiritual condition. From this position of sudden and enormous church attendant growth, Dr. Warren convinced the traditional churches that they would not exist unless they changed to the new purpose driven church, contemporary church worship service. The purpose driven church movement has taken over a large percentage of the autonomous type churches: Southern Baptist, Nazarene, Assembly of God, Pentecostals, Independent Baptists, and other non-aligned Protestant churches. Another reason given for accepting the PDC format by churches has been to get teens interested in attending church. The result has been highly questionable as George Barna, in his book *Third Millennium Teens,* reported: ". . . 63 percent of Christian teens said they believed Muslims, Buddhists, Christians, and Jews pray to the same God."

Dr. Warren depreciates doctrine for the sake of unity in enlisting 400,000 churches into his purpose driven church denomination. He stated:

> We now have "purpose driven" churches in 122 countries. And if I were to ask every "purpose driven" church in America to raise their hand, it would shock America because we don't tell them to change their label. On the front is says, "Lutheran, Second Methodist, Holy Power Episcopal, you name it; Four-Peas-in-the-Pod Four Square"—it's got everything! Every name you can imagine. And we have Catholic "purpose driven" churches. . . .

And I don't make any apology in saying to you that the "purpose driven" paradigm is the operating system of a 21st century church. I believe that because we now have 36,000 case studies, and it's in every country.

And so it doesn't demand that they change from being Lutheran or Methodist or Nazarene or Assembly of God or Baptist or whatever. I don't really care what your *doctrine* is. What I care about is, do you have a process by which you bring people into membership, build them up to maturity, train them for ministry, send them out on a mission, for the glory of God?

—*Foundation* Magazine, Nov.–Dec. 2004

One reason that Dr. Warren uses the newer versions of the Bible is that the word "doctrine" is practically removed out of all of them. Yet the Bible stresses that doctrine is not only important, it is essential: "Whosoever transgresseth, and abideth, not in the *doctrine* of Christ, hath not God. He that abideth in the *doctrine* of Christ, he hath both the Father and the Son" (2 John 1:9).

Dr. Warren is quoted in the *Florida Baptist Witness* (May 6, 2004) as stating, "I intend to use the purpose driven movement to fulfill PEACE in a new reformation."

In other words, Dr. Warren considers the churches that have adopted his PDC format as his own properties to use as he may see fit. He is further quoted by *Time* (November 1, 2005) as stating:

Well, as I said, I could take you to villages that don't have a clinic, don't have. . . . But they've got a church. In fact, in many countries the only infrastructure that is there is religion. . . . What if in this 21st century we were able to network these churches providing the . . . manpower in local congregations. Let's just take my religion by itself. Christianity . . . The church is bigger than any government in the world. Then you add in *Muslims,* you add in *Hindus,* you add in all the different religions, and you use those *houses of worship* as distribution centers, not just for spiritual care but health care. What could be done? . . .

Government has a role and business has a role and churches, house of worship have a role. I think it's time to go to the moon, and I invite you to go with us.

At the Religious Newscasters Association convention in September 2005 Dr. Warren stated:

In the 1990s I trained about a quarter of a million pastors. It's now gone, as I said, to over 400,000 . . . and we're talking about all kinds of different groups, including priests in the Catholic Church, and including rabbis. . . . So anyway, then in the 21st century I said that now we're going global.

Included in Dr. Warren's world peace plan will not only be purpose driven churches from every denomination, including the Catholic Church, but also Hindus and Buddhists temples and Moslem mosques. And we would wonder what Dr. Warren is going to do with the pope, or is he going to be the pope of all religions? It would certainly sound as though this may be part of his peace plan to bring in the Kingdom of Heaven. It would also appear that the 400,000 pastors of PDC churches will have nothing to say about this. And besides, if these 400,000 pastors had to be trained by Dr. Warren they must have been dumb to waste their time going to seminaries.

Dr. Warren states that there will be people from all religions in his purpose driven world, including Catholics, Muslims, Buddhists, and Hindus. However, he has also made it plain that FUNDAMENTAL-ISTS will be excluded.

An item in the *Philadelphia Inquirer* dated January 8, 2006, referencing Dr. Warren, stated in part:

Warren predicts that fundamentalism of all varieties, will be "one of the big enemies of the 21st century. Muslim fundamentalism, Christian fundamentalism, Jewish fundamentalism, secular fundamentalism—they're all motivated by fear. Fear of each other."

At the Aspen Ideas Festival in July 2005 Dr. Warren seemingly referred to Christian fundamentalists as a vanishing breed:

> I could count the number of true fundamentalists on a couple hands today. There really aren't that many left. It's a team that's pushed around, but they happen to be on the media, okay. They happen to be on the media a lot. But evangelicals simply are those who would say we believe in a personal relationship to God. And it's not a denomination. There are Catholic evangelicals, which surprises people. . . . There are evangelicals in every denomination. It is not a denomination. But it is a—the focus is more on relationship than religion."

When Dr. Warren is quoted verbatim his thoughts may appear moronic or oxymoronic. His brain appears to be thinking faster than his mouth can speak. Nevertheless, he does seem to really know what a Christian fundamentalists is, and that he is not one of them.

Dr. Warren stated on May 23, 2005, at the Pew Forum on Religion and Public Life:

> The word "fundamentalist" actually comes from a document in the 1920s called the Five Fundamentals of the Faith. And it is a very legalistic, narrow view of Christianity.

The five fundamentals of the faith to which Dr. Warren objected are:

1. The inerrancy and full authority of the Bible.
2. The virgin birth and full Deity of Jesus Christ.
3. The bodily resurrection of Jesus Christ from the dead.
4. Christ's atoning, vicarious death for the sins of the world.
5. The literal second coming of Jesus Christ.

Are we to believe that Christians who hold to these basic foundational doctrines of the Christian faith are narrow and legalistic? According to the New Testament definition, those who believe otherwise are not Christians.

True membership in the church that Jesus Christ shed His blood for can only be by being born again by faith through grace. Signing a card for membership in a purpose driven church will not get a sinner into Heaven. Dr. Warren (referenced in *In the Name of Purpose*) said that unbelievers on the church rolls become the responsibility of the pastor, and Jesus Himself said to let the tares and the wheat grow together and He would do the separating at judgment. This is just another example of how the Scriptures are being misinterpreted to justify the secularization of the churches.

It is difficult to capture the definitive statements or outlines as to what Dr. Warren actually believes. He may say that he believes that the sinner is saved by faith through grace in Jesus Christ, but then add something else to satisfy the Calvinists or Armenians or Catholics or Muslims, etc. The best description I can give is that he is a supreme pragmatist. He believes whatever his listenership or readership wants him to believe.

A. S. Tozer in *Pragmatism Goes to Church* wrote:

For the pragmatist there are no absolutes. . . . Truth and morality float on a sea of human experience. . . .

It ["pragmatic philosophy"] asks no embarrassing questions about the wisdom of what we are doing or even about the morality of it. . . . When it discovers something that works it soon finds a text to justify it, "consecrates" it to the Lord and plunges ahead. The scripturalness of things or even the moral validity of them is completely swept away. You cannot argue with success. The method works; ergo, it must be good.

The weakness of all this is its tragic shortsightedness. . . . It is satisfied with present success and shakes off any suggestion that its works may go up in smoke in the day of Christ.

Dr. Warren occasionally quotes Charles Spurgeon to justify some of his ideas and programs that undergird the purpose driven church program. Yet, if Charles Spurgeon were alive today, he would challenge Dr. Warren as the chiefest of apostates. In *The Essence of Separation,* Spurgeon wrote:

> A chorus of ecumenical voices keep harping the unity tune. What they are saying is, "Christians of all doctrinal shades and beliefs must come together in one visible organization, regardless. . . . Unite, unite!"
>
> Such teaching is false, reckless and dangerous. Truth alone must determine our alignments. Truth comes before unity. Unity without truth is hazardous. Our Lord's prayer in John 17 must be read in its full context. Look at verse 17: "Sanctify them through the truth: thy word is truth." Only those sanctified through the Word can be one in Christ. To teach otherwise is to betray the Gospel.

In *Feeding Sheep or Amusing Goats,* Spurgeon wrote:

> The devil has seldom done a cleverer thing than hinting to the church that part of their mission is to provide entertainment for the people, with a view to winning them.
>
> Beware of the leaven of worldly pleasure, for its working is silent but sure, and a little of it will leaven the whole lump. Keep

up the distinction between a Christian and an unbeliever and make it clearer every day. . . .

Another purpose driven mission of which Spurgeon would not agree is the church being responsible for feeding and governing the world. We are to live peaceably within nations and pray for those in political authority, not take over their jobs (1 Tim. 2:1–3). Yet, Dr. Warren meets with the Council on Foreign Relations and politicians around the world, trying not to get stepped on, like a mouse in a room full of nervous women. What an exercise in futility.

If the Dominion Now peas and the Dominion Now beans would get together in the Vatican pod, perhaps this Babylonish conglomerate would come up with a person who could control the world. But would not this world dictator be the Antichrist?

We read in Genesis, the sixth chapter, that when the world population increased over the face of the earth, violence increased to an intensity that God had to destroy that generation. I was watching a TV production of "Science" this past month, and the geneticists produced evidence that the DNA structure of the human race indicates that at one time in the distant past the entire world population was destroyed with the exception of only a few individuals. The Lambert Institute reports that the world population today is approaching that at the time of the flood.

I shared with our constituency recently how my little tract, "Is Your Church Going Purpose Driven? How Can You Tell?," was helpful in keeping one of the largest churches in the nation from going purpose driven. And, we have heard from many others where the information we have provided has prevented other churches from making this mistake. I believe we have been very effective, as a national ministry, in challenging, on both a general and church basis, the contemporary church growth movement. However, the PDC continues to spread throughout the world on both a denominational and independent church basis.

The largest complaint we receive is, "Why are you spreading hate and dividing our churches?" But God's Word commands that Christians separate from unbelievers in matters of faith and fellowship—"what fellowship hath light with darkness?"—"come out from among them and be ye separate"—"be not unequally yoked with unbelievers." It is not conservative and fundamental Christians who are dividing the churches; it is the new contemporary PDC members and Dr. Warren who are dividing the churches. So, *quo vadis,* PDC. World Peace? Or, is this the false peace that will result in the judgment of 1 Thessalonians 5:1? Are we on the forefront of the "great falling away" that Paul said must come before the Antichrist is revealed to the world? This is a question to which we may have the answer, very soon.

No pope, no emperor, no political or ecclesiastical organization, including the United Nations and the World Council of Churches, has had the wisdom or means to change the course of exponentially increasing problems of the human race that continue with exponentially increasing populations. Dr. Warren's scheme to combine purpose driven churches with Muslims, Hindus, Buddhists, and atheists to eliminate world hunger, famine, war, disease, and crime is just another delusion and those who follow him are deceived.

There is only one government that will able to bring peace to this earth, and this is the Kingdom from Heaven that Jesus Christ, the King of Kings will govern according to Revelation 19–20. Meanwhile, churches should not be involved in this ecumenical nonsense, but continue in the mission of preaching the Gospel to call out of the world a people who will inherit this everlasting Kingdom of the Lord Jesus Christ (Acts 15).

He which testifieth these things saith, *Surely I come quickly.* Amen. Even so, come, Lord Jesus. The grace of our Lord Jesus Christ be with you all. Amen.

—Revelation 22:20–21

Chapter 12

Is Your Church Going Purpose Driven? How Can You Tell?

I received a telephone call in 2006 from a listener to our program who asked me to write a brief summary about what happens in, or to, a church when the leadership begins changing to a PDC format. The caller said church members who may be opposed to a PDC change need something that is brief yet comprehensive.

I immediately set aside what I was doing, and in one hour composed what I thought would be effective. I did not have to do much research, as I had already personally been in a church where such changes had occurred. Our graphic person, Christi, arranged the copy in tract form with some appropriate pictures.

The tract immediately caught on, and I suppose millions have been disseminated since that time. Vic Eliason invited me to participate in a one-hour nationwide radio program on the subject, and our telephones were tied up for a couple of days with callers requesting copies. VCY has done several programs since on the PDC subject, and when the tract is mentioned our telephones are tied up again with callers. I have finally requested other ministries to put the tact on their websites and encourage their constituencies to duplicate it for distribution. I have hundreds of requests for permission from foreign countries to duplicate it or put it on websites.

In my opinion, this has been the most effective item produced to keep churches from going purpose driven. This tract unveils the secret process hidden from the church members in which a traditional church is practically stolen and changed to a purpose driven church. The following is the text of this tract:

> In the past ten years a large percentage of churches in America, and in other countries, have changed from a traditional New Testament church model to a contemporary purpose driven model, many with sorrowful results.
>
> Contrary to purpose driven church proponents, millions have been leaving their churches after the change occurred.
>
> It is important that every church member know if their church is targeted for a purpose driven church takeover.
>
> Initially, a small clique of church staff, possibly including the pastor or a new pastor, plans the change without telling the rest of the church membership.
>
> Church Transitions, an associate of Saddleback Church in California, trains the clique initiating the change in eight published steps. The church membership is not to be informed of the transition until the fourth step. After the sixth step in the process of change, if there are some in the church who voice concerns, the following is suggested:
>
> 1. Identify those who are resisting the changes;
> 2. Assess the effectiveness of their opposition;
> 3. Befriend those who are undecided about the changes;
> 4. Marginalize more persistent resisters;
> 5. Vilify those who stay and fight;
> 6. Establish new rules that will silence all resistance.

This means the church membership is not told until it is too late to make a difference. In other words the members either accept the changes, or leave the church, which they may have served and given to build.

Dr. Rick Warren, author of *The Purpose Driven Church* and *The Purpose Driven Life* has stated: "When you reveal the vision to the church, the old pillars are going to leave. But let them leave . . . they only hold things up."

Dr. Warren is right in one way. It is the senior members of the church who do indeed hold a church up and keep it from falling into apostasy. While some PDC initiators may not implement the full PDC format, generally these are the signs indicating that your church may be targeted for a purpose driven church format:

1. Change in music to a contemporary rock style.
2. Removal of hymn books; eliminating the choir.
3. Replacement of organ and piano with heavy metal instruments.
4. Repetitive singing of praise lyrics.
5. Dressing down to casual attire.
6. Eliminating of business meetings, church committees, council of elders, board of deacons, etc.
7. The pastor, or a new leader with a few assistants, usually four, takes charge of all church business.
8. A repetitive 40–day purpose driven church study program stressing psychological relationships with each other, the community, or the world, begins.
9. Funded budgeted programs are abandoned, or ignored, with ambiguous financial reports made.
10. Sunday morning, evening, and/or Wednesday prayer meetings are changed to other times; some may even be eliminated.

11. Sunday school teachers are moved to different classes, or replaced by new teachers more sympathetic with the changes being implemented.

12. The name "Sunday school" is dropped and classes are given new names.

13. Crosses and other traditional Christian symbols may be moved from both the inside and outside of the church building. The pulpit may also be removed.

14. In accordance with Dr. Warren's instructions, new version Bibles are used; or only verses flashed on a screen are referenced during regular services.

15. purpose driven church films, purchased from Saddleback, precede or are used during regular services.

16. The décor, including the carpets, may be changed to eliminate any resemblance to the former church.

17. The word "church" is often taken from the name of the church, and the church may be called a "campus." Denominational names may also be removed.

18. An emphasis on more fun and party sessions for the youth.

19. Elimination of altar calls or salvation invitations at the close of the services.

20. The elimination of such words as "unsaved," "lost," "sin," "Hell," "Heaven," and other gospel verities from the pastor's messages.

21. The reclassification of the saved and lost to the "churched" and "unchurched."

22. The marginalizing, or ostracizing, of all who are not avid promoters of the new purpose driven program.

23. Closed meetings between the pastor or chosen staff members without any reports made to the general membership.

24. Open hostility to members who do not openly embrace the new program, or who may have left for another church.

What You Can Do

If your church is in the initial stages of change (music or the first 40-day program), your church could be saved by talking to other church members, and with activist intervention by 10–20 percent of the membership. If nothing is done at this early stage, then by the time the program advances to step four, there is little that can be done except look for another church. Your church has become a purpose driven entity in association with Saddleback Church of Orange County or Willow Creek of Chicago.

You must educate yourself, and others, so that you can mobilize the membership to effectively resist. "For God hath not given us the spirit of fear; but of power, and of love, and of a sound mind" (2 Tim. 1:7).

Dr. Warren in his world peace plan has stated intentions of sending one billion Christians into the world to eliminate human problems. The number one characteristic of a cult is a messianic, charismatic leader.

Purpose driven church books are published by Zondervan, one of Rupert Murdoch's many properties, including 175 newspapers and international television and satellite communications, including in China. Various reports indicate he is building his third wife, Windi Deng, a 22,000-foot mansion in the Forbidden City in Beijing.

Dr. Warren stated on May 23, 2005, at the Pew Forum on Religion and Public Life: "The word 'fundamentalist' actually comes from a document in the 1920s called the Five Fundamentals of the Faith. And it is a very legalistic, narrow view of Christianity."

The five fundamentals of the faith to which Dr. Warren objected are:

1. The inerrancy and full authority of the Bible
2. The virgin birth and full Deity of Jesus Christ

3. The bodily resurrection of Jesus Christ from the dead
4. Christ's atoning, vicarious death for the sins of the world
5. The literal second coming of Jesus Christ

Are we to believe that Christians who hold to these basic foundational doctrines of the Christian faith are narrow and legalistic? According to the New Testament definition, those who believe otherwise are not Christians.

To start a purpose driven church or change to one with the full knowledge and consent of the membership is one thing, but to practically steal a church from Christians who have given and served to build it without their knowledge or consent is quite another.

Don't be fooled by the Saddleback website. You don't catch many fish unless you have a look-alike bait!

At present, it is unknown to me what percentage of different denominations or church groups have adopted the purpose driven format and message. From my own observations, most of the Assembly of God and Church of God churches have gone purpose driven, as well as most of the Nazarene churches. I also would estimate that at least fifty percent of the Southern Baptist churches have gone PDC. I would point out that some in the preceding categories, as well as many on the PDC fence have adopted parts of Dr. Warren's programs without converting to his most overt changes. I would also note that most Independent Baptist and Pentecostal churches have either gone purpose driven or become PDC tainted. While some Presbyterian, Lutheran, and Methodist churches have gone purpose driven, the percentages are not as great as in the aforementioned churches. The old-line Protestant churches have their own eschatology for bringing in the Kingdom. The one denomination that has the fewest changes to the purpose driven format is the Baptist Bible Fellowship, at least from my own observations and information.

What has amazed me more than anything else about the PDC paradigm shift is that evangelical churches and pastors that I have known, whom I thought were solid doctrinal bastions of strength, have fallen for this PDC, "Kingdom Now" brand of Christianity.

Most church memberships on an individual Christian basis do not want to cause division in their church, or to touch "God's anointed" pastor. Most pastors who decide to take their church down the PDC trail capitalize upon this misguided instinct of the memberships. The pastor, usually, has self-centered reasons for making the change. There is really only one service a week in which he has to prepare—the one for Sunday morning for ten or fifteen minutes, with a repeat in the second service if the church has a twin morning service, but no service Sunday evening or Wednesday evening, and only a few intermittent duties in the week. Usually, the pastor will no longer have to be concerned with deacon boards and various committees. Changes have been made in the church staff and he now has the option to choose his own personal attendants, usually four in number. He is no longer pastor in the biblical sense, but the CEO of the marketing corporation. So, the membership should not consider the pastor of a PDC church in the traditional biblical sense.

A PDC Accountable Example

Some of the books and materials we have published at Southwest Radio Ministries that take exception to the purpose driven church message and models have been successfully used to prevent the change in some churches.

Dr. Bobby Welsh, past president of the Southern Baptist Convention, was pastor of the First Baptist Church at Daytona Beach. In 2006 Dr. David Cox became pastor of the church. Dr. Cox evidently moved to change the church to a purpose driven model, which incurred displeasure among the congregation. Some of the members duplicated my tract, "Is Your Church Going Purpose Driven? How Can You Tell?"

and distributed it to the membership. Dr. Cox wrote an eleven-page critical review, attached one of my tracts to the cover, and wrote: "The author of this tract is paranoiac, ignorant, and un-Christian."

When I received a copy of Dr. Cox's article on a Tuesday, I was highly amused, as I am used to such criticisms. But on the following Thursday, the *Baptist Press* carried a large a large headline, **"Dr. David Cox, Pastor of the First Baptist Church of Daytona Beach, Resigns."**

The *Christian Post*, in a story dated January 27, 2007, **"Baptist Megachurch Pastor Resigns Over Controversy,"** reported in part:

On Sunday, a Southern Baptist megachurch in Daytona Beach, Fla., will have an empty pulpit. Instead, a videotape of the church's former pastor will be playing for the congregants as the church currently stands without a senior pastor. . . .

While details of the "difficulty" at First Baptist were not disclosed in [Dr. Cox's] statement or by church staff when called for comments, the Associated Baptist Press reported the controversy was over changes Cox instituted in the church's worship style, his spending habits, and the resignations of many longtime staff members after he took the helm that former Southern Baptist Convention president Bobby Welch retired from in August of 2006. . . .

At a town hall style meeting earlier this month, according to the Daytona Beach News-Journal, Cox stood in front of congregants defending his job as church members vented frustrations over the renovated altar and misplaced priorities under Cox's leadership.

The altar was modernized with a hardwood stage, twin movie screens, and music equipment, but no cross—renovations that congregants saw as excess, especially as the church plans to move to a new church in some three years. . . .

The congregation also complained about the departure of at least five staffers and questioned the salaries for Cox and other staff at the cost of many popular programs in the church. Congregants were also unhappy with Cox's use of the bestselling *The Purpose Driven Life* by Rick Warren and the more contemporary sound of music.

While some defended the changes in the church geared toward appealing to youth, many congregants had begun circulating a petition in the first week of January to dismiss Cox. . . .

Is It Wrong to Protest?

I have occasionally exchanged e-mails with the pastor of my former church, some friendly, some not-so-friendly. In one e-mail he said that he made a lot of mistakes, but he could not go back and undo them. Once a church changes to purpose driven, it is difficult to change back. My former pastor has restored the organ and piano, the choir, a more evangelistic message, and a closing altar call to the unsaved. As I pass the church on Sunday morning going to my regular church now, it appears the attendance is only about one-third to one-half what it once was. The rest of the week, there appears to be little if any activity. It makes me sad to think what has happened to this once Spirit-filled, soul-winning church of thousands of happy Christian families. As far as I am concerned, Dr. Rick Warren and Dr. Bill Hybels destroyed my church. Once a church changes, the members who left will not come back.

I do receive some reports where changing to a purpose driven format has brought in a significant number of new members, but I receive even more reports where the reverse is true. Most church members find it easier and less stressful just to change churches, but anymore, there are not many options. Or, the only other option is to stay home and read the Bible, which may be far better. I personally applaud the membership of the First Baptist Church of Daytona Beach, who cared enough to save their church from a tragic mistake.

Chapter 13

Designer Church/ Designer Heaven?

According to Dr. Rick Warren's first book, *The Purpose Driven Church,* when he went to Southern California to establish a church, he went to the homes of the "unchurched" and took a survey as to what kind of church they would attend. Throughout the four hundred pages of this book, Dr. Warren methodically and systematically explains in detailed accounts how he designed Saddleback to attract, hold, and convert the unchurched to supporting church members. This process included everything from seating, to decor, to music, to air conditioning. I will have to admit that what Dr. Warren did seems reasonable at first, but we read in Proverbs 14:12 that not always does the way that seems right end up in the right place.

In the book of Acts, and even in the epistles to the church, we read little, if anything, about the building of churches, seating, music, or programs. The unsaved were added to the church after they believed the gospel and were born again by faith through grace. Many of the early local churches were in the homes of Christians. Even the first eight thousand members in Jerusalem met in homes for food and fellowship. The epistles to the churches by Paul, John, James, and Peter dealt with the Christians' moral conduct, purity of the gospel message, false teachers, church order, services, fellowship, and witness. The construction of buildings with the additions of pews, pulpits, choirs, and orders of service came later as traditional additions to worship. Most of these additions came by the leading of the Holy Spirit, but some through vanity and imagination. The one thing we need to know about all this is that Jesus said He would build His church, and only the Christians in the local church or assembly belong to Jesus Christ.

When Dr. Hybels was interviewed at his Willow Creek church on television, the interviewer remarked that the church looked more like a night club. Dr. Hybels responded, "We designed it that way." In *The Purpose Driven Church,* Dr. Warren stressed repeatedly that he specially "designed" Saddleback to make the "unchurched" feel "comfortable." This is why pastors who are changing from the "traditional" to "purpose driven" change the decor to that of a nightclub, casino, or bar. The unchurched who are used to going to such places must be made to feel comfortable or at home. This is also why the pulpits, crosses, and other emblems that identify with the Bible or God must be removed. The cross is an offense to those who perish (Gal. 5:11); therefore, the cross must be removed from purpose driven churches.

Not many of the elderly go to nightclubs, beer joints, or casinos; therefore, it is best to get rid of "those old pillars, who only hold things up." They make the "unchurched" uncomfortable.

And, of course, to change the music is a must in a purpose driven designer church. Dr. Warren has stated repeatedly that there is no such thing as Christian music, there are only Christian lyrics. Dr. Warren was once a rock musician in his college days, so he knows he is not telling the truth. You do not hear "Amazing Grace" in a casino. You hear music that makes the gamblers put more quarters in the slot machines. You do not hear "Nearer My God to Thee" in a beer joint. You hear music that will make the customers buy another bottle of beer. Customers in a house of prostitution do not hear "The Old Rugged Cross." In places frequented by the worldly, you hear music that will make them do more of what they should not be doing in the first place.

I am not saying that these things take place in a purpose driven church, but the changes that take place in music, decor, and furnishings identify the type of people who will be more apt to be attracted to such churches. It may be claimed that this is a good thing, as the churches are bringing the unsaved to places where they can be saved. But it is questionable if the lost can be converted where sin is not condemned, Hell is not preached, and repentance is not proclaimed (1 John 2:15–17).

God gave the builders of the tabernacle a blueprint for the true temple in Heaven. Every item in the tabernacle related to the glory and salvation offered to mankind in the sacrifice of Jesus Christ for the sins of the world. In various ways the furnishings and worship in the traditional churches are based for the most part on this great example and truth. So what we identify today as the "traditional" church is much more than just tradition. Some churches are more spiritual and gospel-centered than others, but most at least try to be identified with foundational biblical truths. Since most churches are at least trying to follow the example of the true temple in Heaven, then if the traditional church is to be redesigned, what about a designer Heaven?

A Parody

Let us assume that Michael and Gabriel were discussing why more human beings were not interested in going to Heaven. The conversation went something like this:

in Heaven

Gabriel You know, Mike, the human race is increasing over the face of the earth as it did before the flood; and as it was in the days of Noah, only a very small percentage seem interested in going to Heaven. Perhaps we should go down and find out why.

Michael That seems to be a good idea, Gabe. I've noticed that a lot of people like to go to baseball games, football games, soccer games, and all kinds of sporting events. Why don't you go down to some of the largest sports stadiums and see what it would take to get all those fans to want to go to Heaven.

on Earth

Gabriel Hello Dallas Cowboys football fan. I see that you like to go to football games, but you don't seem to really want to go to Heaven. Why not?

Fan Well, I am really not interested in Heaven because I have not read or heard about any football games, basketball games, tennis games, or any other kinds of sports events in Heaven. That is why I am not interested.

Gabriel Well, if we have large stadiums in Heaven where you could watch sports for the first ten thousand years, would that change your mind about going to Heaven?

Fan Oh, yes, that would be great.

Gabriel I will make a note of that.

later, in Heaven

Michael Well, Gabe, how did you make out?

Gabriel I learned that if the Lord would plan to include a lot of sports stadiums and other facilities in Heaven, and scheduled a non-ending football game between the Dallas Cowboys and the Washington Redskins, a lot of people would want to go to Heaven. And, while I was on earth, I noticed an awful lot of people were going to casinos and places like Las Vegas to gamble. Why don't you go down to earth and interview some of them and find out why they are not interested in going to Heaven.

on Earth

Michael   Young man, why are you so distressed and unhappy? This place of chance makes you so sad, why do you come here?

Gambler   Oh, I just love to gamble, but I just lost last week's paycheck and I don't have any money now to pay my rent. By the way, you look a little strange. Where are you from?

Michael   I am from Heaven. Have you ever thought about going to Heaven when you die?

Gambler   No, not really. I really don't think I would like it there. It's not my thing.

Michael   What if we had casinos in Heaven where you would never run out of poker chips or quarters to put in the slot machines?

Gambler   Oh, I would love that. And, maybe you could slip in a lottery or two.

Michael   I will make a note of that.

later, in Heaven

Gabriel   Well, Mike, did you convince all the millions of people going to casinos and gambling resorts to think about going to Heaven?

Michael   Oh, yes, most of them said they would be very happy to go to Heaven if we would just have places where they could play roulette, poker, bingo, and the slot machines forever. And, as long as as we are on this subject, I noticed that most of the younger human beings like to go to music-type rock concerts. They also spend a lot of time watching or listening to this blatant type noise on TV or what they call CDs. Their minds seem to continually be on this without any time to think about going to Heaven. Gabe, why don't you go down and see about changing their minds.

on Earth

Gabriel   Could I speak to you, young couple, for just a minute. I know you are tremendously interested in listening to these, shall we say, musicians, but I have something very important to ask you. I know you young people like this type of music and coming to this type of gathering, but have you ever thought about going to Heaven?

Young Couple   No, not really. In the first place, we don't care much for harp music, and singing psalms and sitting around shouting "Holy, Holy, Holy, Lord God Almighty," doesn't appeal to us. Also, too many old folks are going to Heaven, and we would really like to be with those of our own age and those who like what we like.

Gabriel   Well, the old folks when they get to Heaven won't be old anymore.

Young Couple	Maybe so, but they will still have the same old negative ideas about what we like to do.
Gabriel	But what if we had Elvis Presley, the Beatles, Jimi Hendrix, and all the major rock stars doing concerts in Heaven for the first million years. Would you like to go to Heaven then?
Young Couple	Oh, yes, that would be really nice. Just put those old, gripey folks in a section by themselves.
Gabriel	I will make a note of that.

much, much later, in Heaven

Michael	Lord, Gabriel and I have taken surveys on earth as to why more human beings are not interested in coming to Heaven. We have found that if You were to redesign Heaven to include all different kinds of sports facilities, bars, nightclubs, and casinos, that more people would be interested in going to Heaven.
Gabriel	Also, You will need to do some redecorating. The rainbow colors are not too popular with many of the people. Harps and trumpets are okay, but we will need to add a lot of drums and heavy metal instruments and speed up the beat of the music. Some that I interviewed suggested a Starbucks Coffee House, but maybe we could get along without that.
Michael	Also, I hate to bring this up, but most of the ones I talked to under the age of thirty thought that those who died over the age of fifty-five should be segregated in a nearby galaxy.

Lord   All these men and women on earth that you interviewed, were they all born again by faith in what I did for them on the cross?

Michael   No, but I think most of them will get around to making that decision in a few million years.

Lord   I am sure you two are well intentioned, but the changes the people on earth wanted have never brought peace and happiness to anyone. And even if they were here, unless they have been changed into new beings with My nature, they would not be happy here anyway. Satan is the prince of the world, and these people belong to him. I love them and died for them just as I died for those who will be with us in Heaven forever, but the way here is by the cross, where I paid the price for sin with My blood. It is the choice of each person to accept this gift or reject it. I created Hell for Satan and all who belong to him: ". . . the fearful, and unbelieving, and the abominable, and murderers, and whoremongers, and sorcerers, and idolaters, and all liars, shall have their part in the lake which burneth with fire and brimstone: which is the second death" (Rev. 21:8).

". . . I go to prepare a place for you. . . . And whither I go ye know, and the way ye know. . . . I am the way, the truth, and the life: no man cometh unto the Father, but by me" (John 14:2, 4, 6).

Chapter 14

Is the Purpose Driven Church Good for Our Nation?

According to Acts 17:26–27, God divided the nations and set the bounds of their habitation. Jesus commanded His disciples in Matthew 28 and Mark 16 to go into all the world, teaching all nations. Those that believed would be saved and blessed, and those that did not believe would be lost.

The apostle Paul went west with the gospel that God gave him to declare to the gentiles, and those nations that have received this message and built their schools, society, and government upon the Person and Gospel of Jesus Christ have generally prospered. Those nations that have not, have not been blessed. The state constitutions of the first thirteen colonies attest to the truth that this nation was established upon the unchanging absolute that Jesus Christ is Lord of Lords and King of Kings. As this nation was settled in every city, town, and community, some of the first buildings that appeared were the local churches. Without the churches and Christian citizens of the United States, it would be difficult to imagine what this nation would be like today.

As the nation's cities have become larger and larger with increasing immigration from non-Christian nations, the relationship of the church to society, and particularly the influence of the churches upon government (state, local, and federal) has changed. And now Dr. Rick Warren claims that the purpose driven church movement is the greatest paradigm shift in "the church" since the Protestant Reformation five hundred years ago. In this I would agree, but is the purpose driven movement, in a national sense, for the better or worse?

Love

Christians are by calling a witness to the lost, suffering, and dying for God's love. As the great shepherd of this paradigm shift in Christendom, is Dr. Warren an ambassador of God's love for the world?

One great problem I have with Dr. Warren's message is that he not only wants to define Christianity, he wants to rewrite the dictionary. He makes up his own definitions. Dr. Warren at Pew Forum stated that there weren't many fundamentalists around anymore. At Vail, Colorado, he said he could count the fundamentalists around today on the fingers of his two hands. A fundamentalist in Christian circles is one who accepts the five fundamentals of the Christian faith. Evidently, Dr. Warren does not love fundamentalists.

On national television Dr. Warren professes that he loves everybody; yet, some dear souls who have worked, prayed, and given to their local church for fifty years are suddenly referred to as old pillars who hold things up. In his book *The Purpose Driven Church,* Dr. Warren indicates that he has gotten rid of thousands of Saddleback members because they would not sign covenants or support the church financially. Dr. Warren thought of Peter Drucker as his model and mentor, but Drucker, while at General Motors, thought of employees as property. The church growth movement seems to operate on the same principle.

Though I speak with the tongues of men and of angels, and have not charity [love], I am become as sounding brass, or a tinkling cymbal. And though I have the gift of prophecy, and understand all mysteries, and all knowledge; and though I have all faith, so that I could remove mountains, and have not charity, I am nothing.

—1 Corinthians 13:1–2

Patriotism

I was born in 1922 and went to school when prayers and reading the Bible in class was acceptable, and even encouraged. In our history and civics classes in both grade school and high school, love of country and patriotic responsibility was not only taught but commanded. I served in WWII, which included three years in combat duty in the South Pacific. Perhaps I am more sensitive to a Christian's responsibility to serve, protect, and pray for our nation than others. Yet I cannot remember hearing anything Dr. Warren has said or written that indicates any love or respect for the United States of America.

As noted in a previous chapter, the Southern Baptist Convention withdrew from the Baptist World Alliance, not only because of liberalism, acceptance of homosexuality, and several other nonbiblical positions in doctrine, but also because the organization was "anti-American." This did not seem to matter to Dr. Warren, as he criticized the Southern Baptists for withdrawing from the Baptist World Alliance, but said that he immediately wrote a check for $25,000 to the BWA.

Government is ordained by God, and governors, congressmen, presidents, and even the policemen are ministers of God in the mission of human government. We are to respect our laws, honor our nation, and pray for all in authority. Certainly, there are many things wrong and evil in our nation, especially today. But even now, this nation is still the greatest nation in the world, and we still have the right to tell the unsaved that there is one Mediator between God and man, the man, Christ Jesus. I may be wrong, but I see little, if any, patriotism in Dr. Warren or the entire purpose driven church movement.

Council on Foreign Relations

Dr. Rick Warren after his somewhat muddled mission to Syria in 2006 tried to justify some of his complimentary remarks about the Syrian Assad regime by saying that he was a member of the CFR and therefore was informed about international affairs.

The Council on Foreign Relations was formed by a collection of internationalists who were disappointed that the United States did not join the League of Nations. All presidents and fifty percent of noted U.S. State Department employees have been members of the CFR since 1945. The Trilateral Commission and the Bilderberger group are part of the CFR's outreaches. The J. P. Morgans and the Rockefellers are the main pillars of the CFR since its inception. Madeline Albright, Tom Brokaw, Maurice Greenberg, Colin Powell, Dick Cheney, Fred Thompson, Condoleezza Rice, Henry Kissinger, Alan Greenspan, Paul Volcker, Jimmy Carter, David Rockefeller, John Rockefeller, Bill Clinton, John Edwards, and John Kerry are just some of the present notable members. A list of members now deceased would include presidents, secretaries of state, billionaires, and international bankers.

Some of the more notable corporations that are CFR members are: Alcoa, Bank of America, Boeing, BP, Chevron, Citigroup, ExxonMobil, Ford Motor Co., General Motors, Halliburton, IBM, Morgan-Chase, Lehman Brothers, Merrill Lynch, Shell Oil, Toyota, and many more.

David Rockefeller, who served as chairman of the CFR for many years, seems to have stated the internal goals of the organization. He wrote in his memoirs in 2002:

Some even believe we [the Rockefeller family] are part of a secret cabal working against the best interests of the United States, characterizing my family and me as "internationalists" and of conspiring with others around the world to build a more integrated global political and economic structure—one world, if you will. **If that's the charge, I stand guilty, and I am proud of it** [emphasis added].

Senator Barry Goldwater said of the CFR:

> Their goal is to impose a benign stability on the quarreling family of nations through merger and consolidation. They see the elimination of national boundaries, the suppression of racial and ethnic loyalties, as the most expeditious avenue to world peace. They believe economic competition is the root cause of international tension.

It is generally accepted that one of the main purposes of the CFR is to erase national boundaries, and considering the combined political, economic, monetary, and communications power within the CFR, this goal is reachable within our lifetime. Considering Dr. Rick Warren's world peace plan, it seems to correlate with the overall program of the CFR.

According to an extended report on the CFR in Wikipedia.org, Robert Pastor, the director of a CFR task force to direct policy on North American affairs, and the author of a book copyrighted in 2001 titled *Towards a North American Community,* has reportedly suggested that the CFR work toward the building of a superhighway between Mexico and Canada, running through the United States. He also seems to recommend the abolition of all national sovereignty and the consolidation of the three countries under one central government. Also included in this CFR report is an item about President Bush and Vicente Fox of Mexico meeting at the Bush ranch on March 23, 2005, where they reached an agreement in the settling of illegal alien concerns that they would be allowed into the U.S. Social Security system, and that as many as sixty thousand Mexican students would attend U.S.

colleges and universities, evidently at taxpayer expense. This agreement seems to have been verified in that the recent illegal alien bill before the U.S. Senate had these items in it. This does not mean that as a member of the CFR that Dr. Rick Warren agrees with this or other policies or directives of the organization; however, I have not read anything he has said or written that indicates that he disagrees.

According to published reports, the CFR has a present membership of thirty-seven hundred of the most powerful men in the world— politically, judicially, and economically. Decisions affecting our nation and the entire world are determined within committees, task forces, and think tanks of the CFR. These decisions are subsequently put into action through legislation, presidential directives, and court decisions. The U.S. Constitution means little if anything today. Dr. Warren has said he is going to use the purpose driven churches to attain certain goals outlined in his world peace plan. Evidently the memberships of these churches have little if anything to say about it. This coincides with standard CFR SOP.

Global Warming Religion

In February 2006 the Evangelical Climate Initiative was established to involve the church in global warming hysteria. Although Focus on the Family and others encouraged Dr. Rick Warren not to endorse this political farce, he and eighty-six other so-called evangelicals did.

Dr. Edward Blick, professor of aerodynamics and nuclear engineering at Oklahoma University, who has also served as meteorologist for the Air Force, has labelled this involvement by clergymen as misguided "global warming religion." It is a known fact that the earth between A.D. 1000 and 1400 was much warmer than it is now. Greenland was called Greenland then because it was green, with farms and vegetation. It is almost solid ice and snow now twelve months out of the year.

Temperatures were higher in the late 1920s and the 1930s than they are today. There were concerns in the 1970s that the earth was headed toward another ice age. Headline notes from the *New York Times* over the last one hundred ten years are as follows:

➤ **February 1895**—"Geologists think the world may be frozen up again. Doomsayers say Canada may be wiped out and lower crop yields will cause billions to die."

➤ **March 1933**—"America is in the longest warm spell since 1776 as temperatures record a 25 years rise."

➤ **June 1974**—"Weather aberrations may be harbinger of another ice age."

➤ **December 2005**—"Climatologists state the ice cores left no doubt that burning fossil fuels is warming the atmosphere in a substantial and unprecedented way."

Temperature variations are caused by solar activity. When temperatures rise or cool on the earth, they rise or fall correspondingly by the same ratio on Mars. Animals breathe in oxygen and emit CO^2 (carbon dioxide). Plants breathe in CO^2 (carbon dioxide) and emit oxygen. If there was no CO^2 in the air, there would be no grass for animals or fruit and vegetables for human beings. The more CO^2 in the air, the more abundant and larger the plants, which in turn emit oxygen and balance the ratio again. This is the way God created perfect environmental control.

According to Dr. Blick, forty-two trillion tons of carbon dioxide is produced yearly by natural causes, most in the oceans. Animals, including human-operated factories and automobiles, produce only three billion tons. That is one part in fourteen thousand. To cut back on farming production, machines, automobiles, and transportation methods would cause a famine that would condemn millions to starvation.

Timothy Wirth, former undersecretary of state in the Clinton administration, stated: "We have to ride the theory of global warming even it if is wrong."

Richard Benedice, special adviser to former secretary-general of the United Nations, Kofi Annan, stated: "A global warming treaty must be implemented even if there is no evidence of global warming."

Dr. Warren in his peace plan has stated that he wants to erase war, famine, AIDS, and other enemies of mankind from the earth. If so, then why doesn't he begin at the doorsteps of Saddleback Church, where there are eight hundred thousand in Los Angeles who are homeless and dying of hunger and AIDS.

Anti-Israelism

I would not charge Dr. Warren or the purpose driven church movement, or the churches involved, with being anti-Semitic. I have not read or heard of anything that would indicate this to be true. However, I am concerned about a lack of support for Israel's right to exist as a nation.

Dr. Warren, like many Protestant clergymen, completely ignores the hundreds of prophetic passages concerning the regathering of Israel out of **all nations of the world.** They embrace "replacement theology," which to them means that the church has inherited all the promises and covenants that God made with Israel. Acts 15 sums up God's plan for Israel. After the calling out of the gentiles a people for Christ's name, He will return and reign on David's throne as promised by the angels at His birth.

During and after World War II, our ministry helped to raise millions of dollars for Jewish relief. I have personally led fifty tours to Israel, and plan to lead my fifty-first in a few months from the date I am updating this book. Israel was given all of the present boundaries, plus Jordan after World War I. Jordan was taken away and now Israel is being divided again. In the 1930s and up through WWII, the Muslim nations in the Middle East so persecuted the Jews that eight hundred thousand went back to tiny Israel because there was no other place to go. The Bible says that when Israel is absent from the land it becomes barren and desolate. When Israel returns, the land blossoms and fills the earth with fruit. This has happened as prophesied. One of my books that is also published in Israel is *25 Messianic Signs in Israel Today*.

Israel's most traditional, biblical, and contemporary enemy has been the nation of Syria. In 1948, 1967, and 1973, Syria joined an alliance of several Muslim nations in attacking Israel without provocation, and for no other motive but to destroy the Jewish State. Before 1967, when Syria was still in control of the Golan Heights, Syrian artillery daily bombarded Israeli settlements at will.

Syria has supplied the Hezbollah terrorist forces in Lebanon with ammunition and explosive materiels for terrorist weapons. Such terrorists during the Reagan administration bombed the U.S. embassy in Beirut twice, killing one hundred, and also the U.S. Marine barracks, killing two hundred forty-one U.S. servicemen. In 1981 our ministry had a Christian program on a radio station in Lebanon near the Beaufort Castle. When in Israel, I would cross over at Metula and go to the radio station. The staff was a couple of Lebanese families. A few Lebanese soldiers manned machine gun emplacements around the station. A few days after my last visit to the station, Hezbollah terrorists attacked and destroyed the station and killed all the staff members, including women and children.

To learn the truth about how Muslim terrorists, with Syrian backing, have destroyed Lebanon and killed tens of thousands of Lebanese Christians, read *Because They Hate* by Brigitte Gabriel.

In November 2006, Dr. Rick Warren visited Syria. Sana, the state agency news, reported:

➤ "Pastor Warren hailed the religious coexistence, tolerance, and stability that the Syrian society is enjoying due to the wise leadership of President al-Assad, asserting that he will convey the true image about Syria to the American people."

➤ "Syria wants peace, and Muslims and Christians live in this country jointly and peacefully since more than a thousand years, and this is not new for Syria."

➤ Warren told Syria's Islamic grand mufti there could be no peace in the region without Syria, and eighty percent of Americans reject the U.S. administration's policies and actions in Iraq.

The International Counter Terrorism organization reported that Syria had supplied terrorist groups in Lebanon with rockets and other weapons of terror to use against Lebanese and Israelis.

In 1978 one of the nations I visited with a 103-member tour group was Syria. In northern Syria we visited the city of Homs (Homa) that had a more Christian population than other cities. We visited a school, and the tour members had a great time with the students. Not long after that, Assad (father of the present dictator) sent his army into the town and slaughtered twenty-five thousand people. Check the encyclopedia for documentation.

Maybe Dr. Warren has visited Israel, and even said some complimentary things about Israel. If he has, I have not read or heard about it.

In its overall effect, I personally do not believe the church growth movement is good for our nation. As Jesus said, let the world take care of its own. Pastors need to preach the Word and take care of the spiritual growth of their membership.

Chapter 15

The Dark Side

To say there is a "dark side" to the purpose driven church movement is indicating that there is also a light side. Many will point out the many "good things" that are the result of the Church Growth movement and the seeker-friendly efforts. If some, especially teenagers, have come to know Jesus Christ and be saved in the PDC churches, then we thank God. But the end result has to be considered. Thousands of churches are being divided; thousands of Christians have been abruptly dismembered from the churches they have supported and loved; the outreach and witness of many churches has been destroyed; and where will it end up? Dr. Warren is not going to be around forever.

The Christian is asked, ". . . What communion hath light with darkness?" (2 Cor. 6:14). The Christian is advised, ". . . have no fellowship with the unfruitful works of darkness . . . " (Eph. 5:11). We read in 1 John 1:5–6, ". . . God is light, and in him is no darkness at all. If we say that we have fellowship with him, and walk in darkness, we lie, and do not the truth."

As Dr. Rick Warren has affirmed, he is leading a Second Reformation. The purpose driven church memberships have studied his books; the pastors have been trained by him in how to change their church into a purpose driven church. The PDC church plays his music; they change their service chronology to his examples; they subscribe to his web sermon outlines. Most purpose driven churches even dress like Dr. Warren, and while they may still have Baptist, Methodist, or Presbyterian on their marquee (and many have already changed), they are Dr. Warren's churches. He is their bishop, leader, pope, or whatever, whether he wants to be or not. Whatever applies to Dr. Warren or his books also applies to the purpose driven churches and their memberships.

I understand that Dr. Warren and purpose driven church pastors and their memberships will disagree with me, but the following are the serious concerns I see in this new religion:

1. **The forty days of purpose:** On page 9 of *The Purpose Driven Life* we read: "Whenever God wanted to prepare someone for his purposes, he took 40 days." This statement had to be made either in ignorance or to deceitfully misinterpret Scripture. Since Dr. Warren must have a doctorate from a major seminary, and we know he attended Southwestern, one of the most credible seminaries in the world, he cannot plead ignorance. We must ask the question, does Dr. Warren set a personal precedent here? "Therefore seeing we have this ministry . . . [we] renounced the hidden things of dishonesty, not walking in craftiness, nor handling the word of God deceitfully . . ." (2 Cor. 4:1–2).

2. **Observing days or any number of days by Christians is heresy:** Dr. Warren makes the unqualified promise on page 10 of *The Purpose Driven Life* to those who study his book, "The next 40 days will transform *your* life." I have talked to many who considered the forty-day study a waste of time, and many churches have experienced no change in conversions or additions after the "forty days of purpose." Churches may determine a specified number of days for a revival or Bible study, but in these instances the emphasis is on the Gospel, not the number of days. Biblical numerics are important to the Kingdom gospel but not the gospel of grace or the church dispensation. Biblical numerics is an entity of the Law,

not grace: ". . . ye desire again to be in bondage [under Law]? Ye observe days, and months, and times, and years. I am afraid of you . . ." (Gal. 4:9–11).

3. **Music:** Individual and congregational singing of hymns and psalms has traditionally and biblically been an important part of worship and giving glory to the Lord (Eph. 5:19; Col. 3:16). One of the most important changes in transforming a traditional church into a purpose driven church is to first switch from traditional church music to so-called Christian rock and heavy metal music. In my former church, the switch occurred two years before it became a purpose driven church. Dr. Warren was a rock musician in the 1960s, the erotic style of music that led the hippie/free love/drug generation to rebel against traditional American and Christian values. Although the words are different, it is still the same music heard today in bars, honky-tonks, casinos, and purpose driven churches.

4. **New Bible versions:** Dr. Warren has encouraged changing to the new versions of the Bible. In *The Purpose Driven Life,* 99.5 percent of the scriptures are from the newer versions, most based on the Westcott and Hort Greek New Testament from the Catholic Alexandrian texts. In the newer versions of the Bible there is an obvious agenda to follow a more general ecumenical terminology. "Hell" is found fifty-five times in the King James Version, but only twelve or thirteen times in the versions that Dr. Warren uses. Likewise, the word "doctrine" is found fifty-three times in the King James Version, but only six to twelve times in the newer versions. Words like "Hell" and "doctrine" cannot be substituted by weaker words, or omitted, and the Word of God still be preserved. Also, it is easier for Dr. Warren to search out the newer, dynamically worded (liberal) translations and find the exact wording he wants to say on a particular subject. *The Message,* one of Dr. Warren's favorite versions, in places even rewrites the words of Jesus.

5. **The Gospel:** The Gospel, the way for an unsaved person to believe on the Lord Jesus Christ, can be found, with some searching, in *The Purpose Driven Life* and perhaps in some of Dr. Warren's other dissertations (ex. p. 58, *The Purpose Driven Life*). But the message of salvation as presented by Dr. Warren has been so compromised and convoluted by qualifications, add-ons, subtractions, and buttressed by references from others whom we would consider heretics and spiritual mystics, that it gets lost somewhere along the forty-day journey.

6. **Doctrinal statement:** As noted in our chapter on "Trying the Spirits of the Purpose Driven Church," Dr. Warren depreciates the importance of doctrine. He seems to say one thing concerning salvation and eternal security, but then will amend it to please those of opposite opinions. The evident objective is to present an ambiguous comprehensive statement of beliefs that will attract as many denominations as possible, where each one can find something that they can agree with. What he may say at Saddleback may be one thing, but to an international religious audience may be another. While Dr. Warren stresses that the sinners, or the unsaved, may be saved by grace through faith, he also stresses oaths, covenants, and tithing, which is frustrating. "I do not frustrate the grace of God, for if righteousness come by the law, then Christ is dead in vain." (Gal. 2:21).

7. **Morality in Christian behavior:** God's chosen apostle to the gentile church, Paul, without reservation or qualification charged Christians to abstain from lusts and sins of the flesh. In his pastoral epistles, Paul also charged pastors and church leaders to exhort their memberships to live righteously before the world. Dr. Warren has openly stated that he does not criticize abortion because he does not want to offend anyone. His support of the Baptist World Alliance by sending a contribution to the organization of $25,000 when the SBC withdrew because of the BWA's approval

of gay marriages, women preachers, and anti-U.S. politics, and then criticizing the SBC for withdrawing from the BWA, speaks for itself. We would think that Dr. Warren needs to read again 1 Timothy, 2 Timothy, and Titus.

8. **Church government and leadership:** Evidently Dr. Warren of Saddleback Church maintains no seminary, nor has he any special authority from major denominational governments or leadership to advise and train laymen, often novices, in how to change their churches or take over leadership of their churches. Yet, this seems to be exactly what Dr. Warren is doing in Church Transitions and various seminars conducted for pastors and church leaders. The purpose driven church movement actually trains laymen in how to change a church from the traditional church, which we understand to be the New Testament model, to a Saddleback model. Often this occurs through a new pastor, or an ambitious assistant, resulting in a dictatorial leader or staff member clique. The dismissal and replacement of other church employees and the absence of financial reports are just a couple of several resulting problems that have been reported. Dr. Warren has been referenced as accepting no responsibility for such changes and/or abuses.

9. **Secrecy regarding change:** One of the most common remarks I hear from Christians who have left their church because it has gone purpose driven is: "We didn't know what was happening until it just happened." Church Transitions, which works with Saddleback and the purpose driven church movement to train PDC staff, teaches that the membership is to be told nothing until the fourth step. It is then that Dr. Warren has said the church will lose the "old pillars." By the time the membership finds out what is going on, the church is already taken over or, we could say, stolen. If there is opposition, then in the sixth step those who are against the change in music, worship, and leadership are to be "marginalized" or invited to leave. Such procedures are unethi-

cal even by secular standards: "And have no fellowship with the unfruitful works of darkness, but rather reprove them. For it is a shame even to speak of those things which are done of them in secret" (Eph. 5:11–12).

10. **Commercialization and marketing:** Certainly, it is true that *The Purpose Driven Life* book and the purpose driven church has a great appeal to the biblically ignorant and to the "make-me-feel-good-quick" churched and unchurched generation of the twenty-first century. However, I contend that the extreme popularity of the book and the PDC movement is due to money . . . money . . . money . . . mass marketing by Rupert Murdoch, the international media mogul and one of the richest men in the world. Even used car dealers offer a bonus copy of *The Purpose Driven Life* with every used car sold. Sam's Club mailed to its vast membership an 8″ x 15″ beautifully designed full-color mailer with the sales pitch: "Count on Sam's Club for a great price on *THE PURPOSE DRIVEN LIFE.*" It is true that Dr. Tim LaHaye's series, *Left Behind*, also sold millions, but it was marketed by mainly Christian-related establishments. *The Purpose Driven Life* book and the related program is being marketed by some who could care less if every soul in the world today went to Hell. "For the love of money is the root all evil: which while some coveted after, they have erred from the faith, and pierced themselves through with many sorrows" (1 Tim. 6:10).

11. **Cultic aspects:** Dr. Warren doubtless abhors the reputation of being a cult leader. Nevertheless there are many behaviorisms in the purpose driven church that appear cultic. Every member of the purpose driven church must read and study his book; memberships change to the type of informal attire that he wears; the music is changed to the music and praise songs at Saddleback; worship patterns and chronologies are changed or patterned after those of Saddleback Church. In my former church, after it went purpose

driven anyone who had a tie or wore a coat was considered out of the church's mainstream and against the pastor. In the epistles to the churches, both men and women are instructed to dress as they like as long as it is modest and honors the Lord. "But if any man seem to be contentious, we have no such custom, neither the churches of God" (1 Cor. 11:16).

12. **Eschatology:** Dr. Warren has much company among ministers and theologians who espouse replacement theology and the A-mil and post-mil positions on the return of Jesus Christ, but he should make it evident that he does not believe in:

1. The separate pre-trib translation of the church.
2. The rise of Antichrist and the seven-year period of Tribulation.
3. Christ's return to reign on David's throne for one thousand years and rule the nations as King of Kings.
4. The Great White Throne Judgment to judge the lost dead of all ages.

Self-Esteem

As expressed by Dr. Warren in the March 2005 *Ladies Home Journal,* to be accepted by God a person should love himself or herself. Yet a study on self-esteem in the January 2005 *Scientific American* reported:

EXPLORING THE SELF ESTEEM MYTH
Boosting people's sense of self-worth has become a national preoccupation. Yet surprisingly, research shows that such efforts are of little value in fostering academic progress or preventing undesirable behavior.

The Gospel message is that God accepts us on the basis of our faith in what His only begotten Son did for us on the cross: Christ's righteousness imputed (transferred) to us to replace our righteousness (net worth—no more than filthy rags).

Message to Youth

The message of the purpose driven church to youth is that church has to be a lot of fun with parties, music, and games. Most teenagers today already have too much "fun": cars, computers, movies, TV, heavy metal music, etc. The church cannot compete with the world in providing "fun."

On page 23 of Dr. Gary E. Gilley's book *This Little Church Went to Market,* we read:

> Growing churches are creating an atmosphere, an environment of fun. So fun has replaced holiness as the church's goal. Having a good time has become the criterion of an excellent, growing church, since fun and entertainment is what consumers want. Yet Scripture references encouraging churches to become havens of fun are, as one may suspect, sadly lacking. John MacArthur observes, "Many Christians have the misconception that to win the world to Christ we must first win the world's favor. If we can get the world to like us, they will embrace our Savior. That is the philosophy behind the user-friendly church movement."

Youth today need to be trained responsibility in the Word of God and the way to mature spiritually as young men and women, the greatest achievement of which is to know Jesus Christ as Saviour and Lord. There are serious concerns as to how the youth programs in the purpose driven church will teach respect for God and His Word as they become adults.

The Disenfranchised

To me the darkest side of the purpose driven church is the thousands and possibly millions of faithful Christians who have served and worshipped in their local church home for years to be told they are no longer needed or wanted. Many, like the hundreds who left my former church, have tried to fit in to other churches, but no church can ever replace the one they left. Many will never go to another church. In the epistles to the church, the elders are mentioned with honor and respect thirty times. If ministers or pastors want to start a purpose driven church, then let them go out and rent a building and start one, rather than turning God's houses of worship into music halls and night clubs.

Paul wrote to Timothy that "in the last days perilous times shall come" when even many in the churches would be "lovers of pleasures more than lovers of God; Having a form of godliness, but denying the powers thereof: from such turn away" (2 Tim. 3:1,4–5).

In chapters two and three of Revelation we find every type of church represented that is in the world today, from the evangelical faith church that is witnessing and watching for the Lord's return (Philadelphia / Rev. 3:7–11) to the rich and lukewarm church that is glorying in its own works and programs (Laodicea / Rev. 3:14–21).

However, Jesus Christ has promised that the "gates of hell will not prevail" against His church. Before the Antichrist appears to form a universal ecumenical apostate church, the true church, all who have been born again by faith in Jesus Christ, will be translated to heavenly places (1 Thess. 4:13–18). ". . . Even so, come, Lord Jesus" (Rev. 22:20).

Chapter 16

A Sign of the Last Days

Many books have been written comparing contemporary events and situations in the political, social, scientific, and military status of the present generation to the signs of the last days given in Scripture. One of my books is on the single prophetic subject of *25 Messianic Signs in Israel Today.*

Paul, the apostle who was called out of season, was given the gospel to preach to the gentiles, those who had no temple, covenant, sabbath, feast days, or promise. Other than foretelling the translation of the church (1 Thess. 4:13–18) and the coming Tribulation (1 Thess. 5:1–4), Paul did not prophesy much about coming events beyond the Church age, the dispensation of grace. It appears to me the reason is that the Christians will not be on earth to take the mark of the beast and go through the Tribulation.

However, the Christians at Thessalonica thought they might be in the Tribulation, because they were undergoing persecution, so Paul wrote to them in his second epistle:

> Let no man deceive you by any means: for that day shall not come, except there come a falling away first, and that man of sin be revealed, the son of perdition; Who opposeth and exalteth himself above all that is called God, or that is worshipped; so that he as God sitteth in the temple of God, shewing himself that he is God.

If the "abomination of desolation" comes before the literal return of Jesus Christ, then there must also be "a falling away" first. The question would normally be raised, "What kind of falling away?" The word in the Greek text for falling away is *apostasia*. In the Geneva Bible, "falling away" is rendered "departure," so either "falling away" or "departure" would have to be understood as falling away from the faith in Jesus Christ, or the departure from the faith in Jesus Christ, or as we could properly say today, the fundamentals of the faith in Jesus Christ. I have already referenced the basic fundamentals of faith in Jesus Christ previously in this book, and I have also referenced several times that Dr. Warren highly disapproves of Christian fundamentalists. It may be disputed that he believes fundamentalists are actually Christians.

According to Paul's epistles to the churches of Galatia, the memberships of these churches are departed, or fallen away from the faith to believe, or deceived by another gospel, which was really not good news but bad news. And although the church at Corinth continued to have problems among the membership with sinful pursuits, Paul still did not charge the membership with falling away from the faith. I understand the letters to the churches in chapters two and three of Revelation to relate more to church types in the last days rather than to the churches of Asia Minor in John's day. It is evident that most of the church memberships of the seven churches of Revelation could be guilty of apostasy, or falling away from the faith.

In First Timothy 4, Paul wrote that in the "latter times," "some" would "depart [fall away] from the faith, giving heed to seducing spirits, and doctrines of devils." Paul explains that this "falling away" would encompass lying, hypocrisy, forbidding marriage, and not eating meat. The falling away that was prophesied by Paul in this letter seems to apply more to the Catholic church than the purpose driven church movement. Of course, Dr. Warren has stated that the Catholics are included in his fellowship of churches and world peace movement.

The apostle Peter in chapter two of his second epistle referenced those "in the last days" who would knowingly and deceitfully deny the return of the Lord Jesus Christ according to their own lusts, or purposes. We are informed in the Bible concerning the world that Jesus Christ will establish when He returns. Evidently the "kingdom now" world that Dr. Warren intends to build is not that millennial Kingdom of Jesus Christ.

Dr. Warren has stated that the purpose driven church model is the first or greatest paradigm shift in the church since the Protestant Reformation. According to the dictionary, a paradigm is a model, often used as a new model, an entirely new treatment for a disease, or even a new model idea, program, or message. Is this why Dr. Warren has such an aversion to fundamentalism? Is this why Dr. Warren also has such an aversion to doctrine? Is this really another gospel, or as Paul would say, a gospel that really is not another gospel, or good news?

I do not say definitely that the purpose driven church is the falling away prophesied by Paul. We do know that before the flood there must have been a great falling away, and Jesus said that as it was in the days of Noah, so it would be again before He returned. The great falling away before the flood resulted in a terrible but just judgment. The same will be true of the falling away just before the Tribulation period, a time that both Daniel and Jesus said would be the most terrible the world had ever experienced or would see again. Therefore, every minister, every pastor, every Christian, is commanded to try the spirits if they be of God. This I have tried to do.

If the purpose driven church is of God, then this book and all others of similar content will have been in vain. If the purpose driven church movement that evidently seeks to unite all segments of Christianity, or purported Christianity, as well as all other religions, is the falling away, or a forerunner of it, then Dr. Warren and his reported four hundred thousand-plus pastoral disciples will have committed the great apostasy that will terminate the Church age.

There is, of course, the possibility that like the New Age religion, the charismatic surge, Promise Keepers, and a few other such false movements, like the Mormons and the Jehovah's Witnesses, the PDC may also stagnate and be overshadowed by a succeeding cultic leader with its own bad news gospel. The supreme order of our day for faithful Christians is not to swallow every religious pill that is offered, but to TRY THE SPIRITS, TRY THE SPIRITS, TRY THE SPIRITS, whether they be of our Lord Jesus Christ or of the god of this world, the devil.

The masses today are looking for a religious leader that will promise peace, security, affluency, and a world without war, disease, or hunger. That man will appear sooner or later than we think. Nevertheless, the faithful in Jesus Christ are commanded to patiently wait for His return from Heaven, the BLESSED HOPE (Titus 2:13).

WITHOUT THIS HOPE, THIS WORLD WOULD HAVE NO HOPE!

Chapter 17

A Final Word

In this book, we have made a serious effort to give a voice to those who have been evicted from their home churches by Dr. Rick Warren's disciples in the purpose driven church movement. We give the final word to a Christian friend who was himself one of these victims:

Dear Pastor Hutchings:

This Sunday marks the first anniversary of our new church and has caused me to reflect on the events of the past couple of years. As you recall, one year ago the leadership of Gardendale (used to be called Gardendale Baptist Church) chose to "remove from membership in the family" those members that did not agree with the statement: Pastor ---------- was the "God-called pastor of the church."

As a deacon, I did not want to vote against my pastor; yet could not bring myself to vote friends, family, and fellow deacons from the fellowship so I resigned my duties and left the church the week of the vote. Members urged the pastor not to have the vote. "If it be possible, as much as lieth in you, live peaceably with all men" (Rom. 12:18).

On July 18, 2004, the vote was held. Since I had resigned I did not attend. Over three hundred people, many of them seniors that had sacrificed years of labor, time, and money to build the church, were voted out. I understand from friends on both sides that it was extremely confrontational and there was an evil, dark presence in the room.

Pastor Hutchings, the changes were so rapid. Within a year and a half:

> The pastor turned the Wednesday night service over to the family pastor and moved it to a small fellowship hall room.
> Home groups replaced the Sunday evening service.
> Business meetings became very rare.
> Additional staff positions were created without the church's knowledge.
> The focus became building attendance over reaching the lost and equipping the saints.
> "It's all about the numbers."
> The sermons became shallow—more practical, conference-type messages
> New members had to sign a covenant to support the pastor.
> Money was raised for certain causes and then used elsewhere.

The church we joined, Brighton Park Baptist Church, was down to just a handful of people. They welcomed the Gardendale exiles with open arms. For a year now we have looked for a pastor. We have found it very difficult to find a preacher not influenced by the purpose driven movement.

We so appreciate the ministry of Southwest Radio Church.

Please continue to warn listeners of the dangers of the purpose driven movement.

> Sincerely,
> David Freymiller
> KCTA Radio Operations Manager

About the Author

Dr. Noah Hutchings serves as president of Southwest Radio Church Ministries in Oklahoma City, Oklahoma. He has been with the ministry since April 1951, the same year he received Christ as Savior and Lord. He has written more than 100 books and booklets covering Bible commentary and prophetic topics. Dr. Hutchings is a member of the University of Biblical Studies in Oklahoma City, and is a member of the Gideons organization.

Kim

I Will Make Darkness Light

1/Ring the Bells 2/Angels We Have Heard on High 3/Go Tell It on the Mountain
4/Silent Night 5/Some Children See Him 6/Down from His Glory
7/Sweet Little Jesus Boy 8/O Holy Night 9/There Is a Balm in Gilead
10/My Heavenly Father Watches Over Me 11/Thanks Be to God
12/Praise the Lord 13/Amazing Grace 14/The Lord Is My Light
15/The Lord's Prayer 16/God Bless America 17/The Holy City
18/Without Him 19/His Eye Is on the Sparrow
20/Song of the Soul Set Free 21/How Great Thou Art
22/Thank You, God, for Jesus
23/I Walked Today Where Jesus Walked
24/No One Ever Cared for Me Like Jesus
25/Jesus Is Coming Again

Kim Wickes was born in Korea. After being blinded by a bomb during the Korean War, she was adopted by an American family. Kim earned a Masters in music from Indiana University. Subsequently, she graduated from the Vienna Institute of Music on a Fulbright scholarship. Kim speaks four languages, and she has sung at Billy Graham Crusades, international Christian conventions, and churches around the world. She is known as one of the finest Christians vocalists of our time.

ISBN 1-933641-17-7

Music CD   Approximately 1½ hours

Retail — $12.95

Ring the Bells

Angels We Have Heard on High

Go Tell It On the Mountain

Silent Night

Some Children See Him

Down From His Glory

Sweet Little Jesus Boy

O Holy Night

There Is a Balm in Gilead

My Heavenly Father Watches Over Me

Thanks Be to God

Praise the Lord

Amazing Grace

The Lord Is My Light

The Lord's Prayer

God Bless America

The Holy City

Without Him

His Eye Is on the Sparrow

Song of the Soul Set Free

How Great Thou Art

Thank You, God, for Jesus

I Walked Today Where Jesus Walked

No One Ever Cared for Me Like Jesus

Jesus Is Coming Again

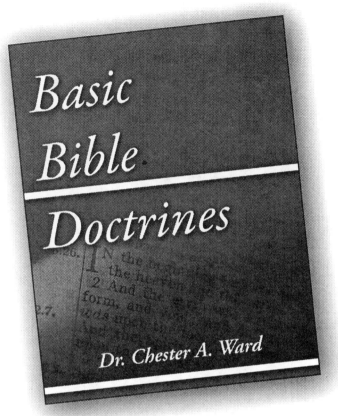

Basic Bible Doctrines is a study guide to help the individual understand the scriptural foundations of our faith.

Each topic is presented in an easy-to-read style using an outline form. Numerous scripture references are included to encourage individual Bible study. A review quiz is given after each lesson as a learning tool.

Basic Bible Doctrines affirms that the Word of God is the eternal truth and final authority in the Christian's life.

ISBN 1-933641-14-2
8" x 11" Paperback   114 pages
Retail — $14.95

In *25 Messianic Signs in Israel Today* Dr. Hutchings outlines signs occurring in Israel that the Bible says will immediately precede the Great Tribulation and the coming of the Messiah. To Christians, this means that Jesus Christ must be coming soon. God is now showing the Jews through these signs what is coming very shortly.

Dr. Hutchings and Mrs. Treibich have put these signs in chronological, documented order so that no Jew can doubt (if he believes the Torah) that before the Messiah comes, a time of great persecution and trouble must come first.

ISBN 1-933641-06-1

Trade Paperback   176 pages

Retail — $12.95